Do you have two and a half hours to spend on you? Perhaps on a plane or train journey, or even six - thirty minute windows where you read, think and absorb the stories and messages in this book.

In this busy world if we could grant one wish to our work colleagues it would be to create the time to think. To think about me and how I develop more control of my life and then the broader context of creating a better work place.

Thinkboxing is a dialogue journey into personal and work related life style themes with views on people dynamics and power players in organisations. We question and explore the ways in which organisations evolve and how our work communities develop an introverted world of their own. Does your organisation work in its own little logic bubble? Someone powerful says - we do this and we don't do that - these ideas then mushroom into behaviours that translate over time into the way it is around here. It's the current and ancient power brokers in your organisation who set and reinforce the standards and behaviours within which you work, and the way it is right now will be a distillation of the successes and failures of the past.

Our work with tens of thousands of working people has given us a valuable insight into how organisations react to the step changes that are often required to move towards a competitive future. We believe that if organisations fail to address the issues of the future early enough in their life cycle they automatically create a performance drag from which they may not recover.

One of our core beliefs is that we can only implement a future that we can describe. In the early chapters we focus on how we describe our world to ourselves and explore the shallow end of why we react the way we do.

Then when you are in charge of your thinking bus we hope that you will step up to the challenge and ask the insightful questions that help your organisation and working environment become a great place to be.

The current performance challenge to old-Europe's organisations is significant. But we do have a history of being world leaders and it was our people who made us world class. We are already destined to lose out in the short term technology stakes. And as investment moves East we will not be able to compete on an equal footing in the new and emerging world of the technology component of work. We can however influence the next wave of investment, if we market our people as world class, as there is nothing to stop us developing the people in our organisations into the competitive advantage, that makes a real difference.

We should honour our organisation's history as we address the issues of the future, and empower the voice of those who can describe a competitive way forward. **This new change curve can start with your description of something different.**

You can influence the route map that guides your organsation's journey into the future. Then when you are future focussed just start working differently with a recognition that when the people who work with you are able to describe something similar, you can all become a force for change.

Now reframe from the change dimension of all of us, our company, our organisation, our industry, to little young me and remember that in your personal world of work and life - **Change starts with me - and my ability to describe a new way, and then my preparedness to move towards it.**

With inspiration and ideas
from the incredibly
talented people that we
are proud to have
worked with.

- We don't intend to tell the story of "feed the world, make it a better place, for you and for me and the entire human race".

- However consistent with the change theme in the Live Aid song, we do want you to make your work environment "a better place for you and me".

- What will it take to make your; office, plant, depot, school, or organisation, one that everyone is proud of?

- What can we do to start the process of creating good and then great places to work?

- We can only progress towards a future that we can describe.

- When employees describe where we are going together, we can move towards it.

■ Thinking about you

■ Leading the opinions of others

■ Memories from yesteryear

■ Managing you today

■ Games organisations play

A great place to work is Happy Bunny territory.

■ Power base changes

■ The importance of moving to a higher order

■ Contents

■ Thought Bubbles

Never judge a book by its cover, there is a good chance that you will misjudge its outcome and purpose. Thought bubbles and thinkboxing is intended to explain a range of observations based on New Era Associates world of work.

Our story is a message from all of us to all of you, to individuals and groups as they progress to teams and onwards to the organisations that people eventually populate. We hope that our experience in helping people and organisations manage change at the sharp end where fears, confusion and uncertainty often influence our world, will help you progress towards understanding.

This study book will hopefully introduce new ideas and perspectives that will help you cope with work life changes and guide your thought systems towards solutions to problems that you may meet at work. How do you deal with the Uh-Oh moments that for some of us, can upscale into Uh-Oh weeks or even months and years. When an organisation has to face up to the need for change then the people who work in it move out of their comfort zones and into confusion very quickly.

One of our associates read the draft of this study book and said you need to explain Uh Oh!! and Thinkboxing from the start. So here we go – Uh Oh is the message that your body sends to tell you that it is not happy. You don't think your way to sadness, do you? It arrives doesn't it? And the emotion is already here when the thought bubble captures it and then explains it to you. Our cover girl is Ella, she has just met Uh Oh!! !!

For the most part ideas emerge very quickly. Just imagine that our ideas are captured by cartoon type thought bubbles, these idea bubbles grow in front of our eyes in the same way as if they had ballooned from the end of the children's soap bubble blowing event. As they drift upwards into the right space, near to your head, they capture the idea that you have just had. All of the thought data is contained inside the bubble, as you peer through the rainbow coloured ball you can see the pictures, hear the sounds, and relive a full sense replay of the event, including the emotions that are associated with the information. When the bubble bursts a magical energy wave downloads the memory on to your neck top computer's hard disk.

As the bubble captures the idea, the event matures into a memory that has a whole body dimension. Your Thinkbox records sights, sounds, smells, tastes and of greatest life importance the emotions that are associated with the event.

When our thinkbox receives incoming data we analyse the information from a full sense perspective. Please take another look at this book's front cover pic. Isn't it amazing how the image communicates so much? I'm confused, worried, not sure about this situation at all, what am I expected to do next, if things don't change, I think I'll cry and see what happens. When the good-feeling thoughts disappear, Uh Oh!! takes over. The sequel to the cover story is that the uncertainty closes with a quick and happy ending. Big sister interprets the signs and says 'I'll come and play with you', breaking up the downward spiral of fear and concern, smiles take the place of the pending tears and good feelings replace the fears. Happy bunny succeeds Uh Oh!! All is well.

Good times replacing not so good can easily be orchestrated for the young. Just a little continued love and support or even the appearance of a face that you know can turn things around. Tears and smiles often used for effect can be milli second fast as they arrive and disappear.

Now fast forward life to the pressure pot time of mid twenties to thirties. Add mortgages and family and career to the Uh-Oh!! cocktail. Friendly faces or comforting words don't help too much now. We tend to swallow Uh-Oh and try to manage it for ourselves, as opposed to looking for help. Messages from the past pop out of our thinkbox 'when the going gets tough the tough get going'. How do we cope with uncertainty and fears now? The emotions are the same as when we were young, but our neck top computer has a great deal more stored in the memory banks. Our thinkbox searches through this data to find the information that will help us clear confusions and move us back into a comfort zone – In the zone, then the world is a great place. This is the world of the happy bunny, everything is OK and this is a great place to be right now, enjoy the moment. Capture the sights and sounds and smells and feelings, hold the soap bubble out in front of you again, you can revisit this data when you need, just recall the happy bunny bubble.

■ Thinkboxing

Is the place where you work a great place to be? Or is it Uh-Oh for most of the working week? If you are a leader in an organisation, or just someone that others depend on for guidance, you will inevitably meet Uh-Oh!! when you and your colleagues experience work related change and the associated pressures that this creates. When change impacts on your work team, where do your work colleagues seek advice? Who do they follow as the change risks start to escalate? Significant changes are accompanied by confusion and when confused our thinkbox hedgehogs. Your brain rolls up into a ball and sticks pricklies out until it thinks its safe to come out again.

If your work colleagues are prepared to listen to you and to follow your ideas and suggestions, your thinkbox has probably developed coping strategies and resources that others may not have, these will help you, help others form opinions on what to do next.

When change arrives lets take it as read that Uh-Oh is something that we have to deal with. Thinkboxing is a set of skills that help us manage Uh-Oh events, perhaps best considered as the brain's equivalent of a martial art. When real kick boxers attack each other they deflect physical force, they train and up skill to a point where they can use the attackers energy to unbalance and off guard the challenger, when skilled you can even turn the attack and aggression to your advantage.

Consider this Thinkboxing example, the American lecturer had just presented his thoughts on why we should incorporate best practice ideas into our new green field business start-up. We moved to question time,that kicked off at the 'have a nice day you all' end of what many people were thinking. Then came the guided missile question, "Mr Achenburger, you have explained how all of these concepts and theories have worked in your American plants and we have all been there and sensed the results. But what was obvious to us was that the American people are very, very different to us Brits. We don't walk down the garden and salute our country's flag in the morning. Now if the people of our nations are so different, then do you think that you can translate what works in America, to down town Inverness?" Silence followed, the question had matured in the telling from a missile question into an arrow to the heart jobbie.

I could see the arrow pinpointing towards the presenter, it was getting closer with each millisecond of the ongoing pause. Then the presenter said, 'Marcus, it was Marcus at the back there wasn't it, that is a really good question, what do you think?' Uh-Oh the arrow was heading straight back to the questioner with a three times upgrade on its velocity.

Marcus had asked what everyone wanted to know. The presenter didn't have an answer and had obviously been asked questions that he couldn't answer before. But with a simple technique, he had deflected the incoming force and created time for a more considered response.

In working life we have many interactions with other people that need consideration or interpretation. The message that we receive from a communication is often more complex than the words that are exchanged. What was Marcus's real intent, what message was he trying to convey? Was the question really a statement, was he actually saying -'I don't think these ideas will work in the UK'? Consider communication as a multi level process, the words exchanged are one level and the meanings exchanged are multi level and more complex.

What message did the presenter receive? He probably thought this guy is challenging the ideas in my presentation. Is this question communicating a belief that I am not being honest or sincere-Uh Oh? Thinkboxing creates the time for a considered response, time to progress towards a more constructive exchange between two people?

They say that great sportsmen have time on the ball or that they seem to create space to play where others don't have this luxury. Thinkboxers are in control of their interactions. By managing themselves through Uh-Oh that little bit better than others they create the time for considered, versus automatic knee jerk type responses. Practice and experience helps, the technique used by Mr Achenburger created time and space for him to think. He could now manage Marcus to a better outcome, did Marcus have an adding value idea, could Marcus improve on the presenter's concepts, or if the words really meant 'these ideas will not work in the UK', then the process had created the opportunity for the discussion of how they could work. There are many occasions when a difference in perspective results in new ideas by exploring the differences in a search for added value. Could Mr A improve on his core concepts if they were amended or changed to fit, in Brit land?

When you manage your thinkbox you create opportunity space for added value exchanges that will help you get the best out of others. Thinkboxers focus on how we can better understand each others opinions with better ideas as the expected outcome.

■ Key Messages

Working life can be easier when you understand you. Understanding arrives when the brain, our neck top computer, presents us with a meaning that makes comfortable sense to us, words, pictures and emotions that combine to form an OK message. We actually live in the world that our thinkbox-describes to us, our thoughts create our reality. How does our Thinkbox work? We process incoming data, translate events, create our own sense and meaning. When our thinking box has sensed the situation before, or processed similar incoming sights and sounds, you are in control and capable, your world of work can be a great place.

How does our thinkbox react when it processes new and especially unexpected data, when the world we live in sends not so good or Uh-Oh!! messages . This is the time when confusion and associated body effects take over. Our whole being moves out of its comfort cocoon and into an uneasy confusion. Muscles tighten, bones become fixed, we may experience a heat effect and the top storey of our body becomes confused this is pressure pot time.

When Uh-Oh arrives, we are often left wondering as to the best way to deal with this situation and circumstance. Part of the answer will arrive when we understand the difference between our in control and OK condition and the not so good and confused Uh-Oh state.

Uh-Oh and the Happy bunny comfort zone have the same thinkbox characteristics. In Uh-Oh mode our thinkbox replays what it remembers of the last time either this or a similar circumstance occurred. It is important to remember that this is old information and for most of us Uh Oh has at least two components, thoughts and feelings. When your thinkbox presses the replay button, old thoughts and feelings track though your mind and body.

I was stranded in a hotel room with a television and hundreds of channels and was aimlessly failing to connect with any of the programmes until an old western flicked on, it had grey and white pictures with voices to match and I instantly zipped back thirty years in the watching. These old pictures and sounds created a warm feeling, as I watched the replay of very old images of bygone times. But this televised replay of old data is no different from a thinkbox replay.

A similar recall process operates when your thinkbox replays decades old data as today's information. They aren't presented as history defined images or old emotions, but as real time today data with the sharp end of the happening manifesting as stomach tightening, or shoulder closing and general body uptightness. In summary this old data has resulted in an unhappy bunny experience today, even though this is just a one more time revisit of old thoughts and feelings.

Uh-Oh or Happy Bunny can become a choice, just as soon as you can explain them to yourself. When you understand these life conditions you will realise how incredibly quickly your mood swings in response to some things of which you are aware, or in some cases just because the thinkbox takes you that way.

I was once a one part, in a five hundred and twenty six part caterpillar queuing to see Peter Pan at Euro Disney. This was a fun park but when you looked at the queue of people you could be forgiven for thinking it was a competition for the longest line of the most miserable mug shots.

The helpful signpost said queue time one hour and thirty minutes. What it really meant was, go now you dummy and come back when it's raining. But I was fully occupied answering my young grandaughters questions and watching Jess work the queue. She had eyes that everyone wanted to talk to, eyes connect with fellow queuers who usually asked the same question, what is your name? This question could take you anywhere, right the way from my name is Jessica, this is my Grandad, through to my mummy doesn't wear pyjamas.

For one hour and twenty minutes of sign posted queue time, we were in happy bunny mode. Disney was a great place for anyone who could walk under one part of the caterpillar and into the next row. Then when the time sign read 'ten minutes from here' the world changed. As we looked towards the entrance a small voice said it's dark in there Grandad and all of a sudden we were covered in salty wet stuff, the sunshine smile was gone, 'I don't want to go in there' but why darling 'because I don't like Captain Hook'. One happy bunny exits stage left and neither Wendy nor Michael with teddy nor Peter Pan on a rope could change the mood. Uh Oh was in control with old, fear and don't like patterns center stage.

Ask a young child to tell you about someone they don't like, in an instant they move from real time now and relaxed into a squeezed eye, I'm angry, pose with an associated full body effect. Don't stay with this data too long, change the logics to someone that they like and watch the frozen features melt into normality.

Now where one Disney queue failed another one succeeded. As soon as I mentioned the chocolate ice cream queue the sun came out and the smile returned but in many respects we were only substituting one set of old data, with a don't like and a fear attached, for another. What goes around comes around in the Uh-Oh world, 'Mummy, Grandad bought me ice cream and lemonade'. Uh-Oh!!.

In adulthood, changing the way we feel is more difficult and can take longer to work, however I am reliably informed that full brain programming from early childhood with the chocolate ice cream bean can speed up the process right the way through to wrinklehood.

Now the thinkbox process is the same for the old as the young, in effect we substitute one thinkbox state the Lo, for another the Hi. Lo has the Uh-Oh feeling and Hi is the happy bunny.

To move the Hi-Lo state process into the choice category we need to take a few simple steps on the path to lots of practice.

First, learn to be able to describe to yourself in words, in your head, what the Hi resource state feels like. Sense measure the whole body effect through the words; my breathing was deep almost measured, my muscles were relaxed, I was looking out over the Loch and everything including the water sparkled, the mountains greyed into the distance, what a back drop, clean air and thoughts to match. Choose your moment, capture the whole sense of this event and hold it out in front of you, just above eyebrow level, wait for the soap bubble, describe the Hi state for yourself and score this in the eight to ten range on your bodyometer.

Then measure the body effects of an Uh-Oh event, stomach tightening, breathing shallow, legs driving into the floor as presenter's panic kicks in. Is this room hot or is it me, don't even ask, you are contributing to global warming. Or sense the unfair verbal attack of a colleague, with an even bigger black edge to the mood cloud if Uh-Oh results from your boss's unfair or unwarranted criticisms. Capture the body effect of this Lo state. You will find that your body is much more rigid than your chair, breathing shallow, many of your body bits are up tight with a full head of Thinkbox confusion built in.

When you can describe both states in words and explain them to yourself, you are now in a position to make a choice. But remember the choice is between one old data based state for another.

We will explore both states and through the simple process of understanding, develop thinking tools that help you manage you through confusion to a clearer view of the world.

When you understand the Happy bunny zone and can interpret the Uh-Oh triggers and effects then you can make a simple choice. Which of these two life conditions do I want to live in at this point in time.

Comfort Zone **Hi**

Surf the wave when
Talent = Challenge

Happy
Bunny
curve

Rock Logic

The way we are has been fashioned over time into fixed response patterns. Very fixed in certain aspects of the way we live and in the way we behave, solid, rock like, logic loops, that influence or dictate how we respond to a situation. The idea that we behave predictably and live to pre programmed scripts may not be one that we are comfortable with. Think through your get up in the morning routines, what do you do first when you get out of bed, then next and then next, are you visiting a sequence and pattern of activity that you repeat day after day. These patterns become so predictable and automatic that you can often complete the drive to work and reflect on how on earth did I get here? I wasn't thinking about turning left or right, as a matter of fact I wasn't thinking about anything to do with driving. Our programmed brains can cope quiet well with life aspects and challenges that we have met and managed before.

Responding in a predictable way is also part of our body's defensive and protective support systems, a self preserving mechanism with programmed responses that can insulate us from shocks and prevent us from repeating some of the hurts of history. Fixed responses help us create an OK umbrella based on our past experience.

Having dealt with this situation in a certain way the last time and it worked, or at the least the issues went away eventually, then we automatically do the same thing again. When we experience changes to this programmed and predictable life environment, and have to face new issues that we haven't met before, one of two things happens; if we enjoy change and new challenges we get excited, but for those of us who don't the most likely outcome is Uh-Oh!!. Our Thinkbox automatically and naturally defaults to Uh-Oh, and probably I am not sure what I should do next. At times like these even a do nothing decision can take too long to arrive.

Oops I've said it, too late to think about a reasoned response now, can often be the result of a poorly managed Uh-Oh event!!

When our experience to date or perspectives are challenged by a new world circumstance, we naturally apply what we know, the old data base is explored to identify a way of dealing with the issues, now if this way works for us we move into happy bunny mode - if it doesn't Uh-Oh takes over.

In the following pages we explore the shallow end of how we think and react and respond. Having explored me and how I function, we then move on to the us equations, how do teams and work groups function. As we move from little-us to the communal thinkbox of all-of-us how do organisations cope with the change agenda of the continually evolving world of work?

When you understand the whole body mechanics of the comfort zone, the Hi and the natural thinking and body reaction to Uh-Oh!!- the Lo, you can start to manage this life situation more effectively. With practice you can then choose to spend more of your time in control of you.

■ You can influence your world of work.

■ Challenged? How you react is important.

■ Can you help those around you move towards order and away from confusion?

■ Rely on your emotional networks to guide instinctive progress.

■ But remember that natural reactions drive from yester years, rock logic data base.

■ Think bubble both Hi and Lo, then choose.

A New Leadership Era

New Era's colleagues and associates work with organisations, groups, teams and individuals as they address the issues of change. Our energy centers on addressing the issues of change ahead of the time and our work with hands-on team members through to board level employees has provided us with the opportunity to learn a great deal. Working with tens of thousands of people in many different businesses through an out of doors, exercise-based, thinking challenge programme, leaves us describing a world of work that is fairly predictable. From Boardroom to Operational teams we see similar patterns of response and behaviour. The way teams form and organise, Leadership characteristics, decision making and problem solving challenges are met with enthusiasm towards similar outcomes. Perhaps one of the most valuable insights from our work has been that given the even playing field that our programme creates, superb Leaders have emerged from all levels in the Organisation.

We were working on the employee testing, interviewing and induction training of a world class component supplier to the automotive industry. They were commissioning a highly automated and complex production system. The early recruits were second-degree graduates who were destined to carry out the proving trials on the new equipment in Europe and then ship and commission the kit to the enormous empty shed that was poised for activity. Our induction programme delegates were going to be a real challenge, bright young sparks for the most part with a pinch of boffin within the mix and a few other raw ingredients in a twenty five delegate group. We would be working with them to start the process of establishing the people part of the performance culture that was to underpin a world competitive business Operation.

The early intro exchanges were guarded and stuffy through the talk and chalk chat. However behaviours changed when the small groups were challenged with the task of neutralizing radioactive isotopes, in an old reservoir, on top of a windy hill. The team could succeed if they implemented a plan to lower a plastic tube on to the top of the isotopes using a rope and bits of bent wire. At least eight delegates should have died from radio active exposure on this exercise as the knowledge base and programming of university degrees and techy thinkboxes invented a whole series of unworkable plans. Uh-Oh and confusion was etched on the cold faces with a think bubble above each head reading - I don't want to look stupid here on my first action day in this new company.

Ropey plans followed dodgy ideas until someone stepped forward and said why don't we do this, he was ignored until the two other untried plans had failed and it was getting dark, so why not. We watched with amazement as the janitor explained what we needed to do. The team then overcame a glue like resolve to stick with the old ideas by quietly implementing their plan in tandem. With the last shakes of freezing hands that marked the death of the last graduate idea, came a silent drift of minds and people to the Janni's plan. For most of the out of doors exercises two or three of the janitors either came up with the ideas or led the action of the team as their practical brains better adapted to the green challenges of the programme.

Just to round out the story the big empty sheds that would house all of the equipment had a high spec smooth, but non-slip and very clean floor. One of the plants performance standards was that this floor would be kept in this condition for as long as was possible. As installed you could have moved all of Scotland's and half of Canada's curling players in for a knees down, this floor was inspiring. Here was the hard evidence that this was a special place and we knew that if we could harness the talent and think power of all of the employees and create an involving people culture, we could be world class.

The janitors were to be the keepers of the floor and many a visiting contractor bearing a twenty-ton machine with wheels was subject to janitorial appraisals. They were of course well supported by the accountable engineer for each piece of kit who understood the Thinkbox potential of the man in the flat cap, who had helped them escape the cold mountain many months before. Respect having been earned through performance and results.

Our change programme has evolved from fifteen years of improvement and was summarised by an associate from ESADE the Business school at Barcelonna University as – learning through failure. Was this a little harsh we pondered, when all we were trying to do was to explore the unexpected and the shallow end of Uh-Oh in a fun environment, as the teams moved towards a successful outcome? The fact is that if you experience and understand what happens when you fail it does help you move towards a successful outcome next time. An understanding of what might work very often spins off from what doesn't work and when we thought through our visitor's perspective, he was right.

On reflection the delegates tell us the programme works for them but there is a significant difference in the way in which the different levels of an organisation cope with the unexpected. Operational teams seem to be the most resilient and flexible, and are blessed with that bounce back ability described by one of our veteran Leaders as the result of us - the management that is – educating them through our inability to get it right first time. When Management teams meet Uh-Oh we know we are in for a bumpy three days.

All in all even the tougher delegate challenges are a priviledge and the harder the issues the more we learn as we very often leave our comfort zones. New Era's learning curve has resulted in the thoughts and models on the following pages being thoroughly tested. They are presented in the hope that they will prepare the reader for many of the predictable and programmable change effects that we have encountered.

Our Purpose is to influence your thinking and help you convert the Uh-Oh's!! of life into a self-sustaining and enriching development opportunity.

As you read through the words and visit the images we hope that your thought process will evolve into a better understanding of you. With an associated recognition that moving out of your comfort zone is part of your life's learning curve.

■ Organisations need talented leaders.

■ We lead by offering opinions others follow.

■ Work teams have Opinion leaders.

■ Through fair means and sometimes foul tactics, power bases are formed.

■ When change creates Uh-Oh who do you turn to, to help clear confusions?

■ For optimum performance organisations need informed Opinion leaders at all levels.

■ Busy people prefer thin books with information delivered quickly

True or False?

Don't try answering the question just yet as there isn't a robust yes or no, stand alone answer. As with most thinkbox outputs the answer depends on the context within which you frame the question. You will need more information to help clear the confusion on a yes or no, true or false, decision. The answer could be False if you categorise an information message as follows

- an information message is something that helps us clear a thinkbox confusion.

Information clears confusion

When confused we all need quick answers so the context helps guide us to an answer. Busy people may not create the time to read, moving us towards a True answer, if we then use the contextual message that information clears confusion, then everyone of us needs information quickly, moving us towards a False answer. Do you find these paragraphs a little confusing? Good, with time and more thought you will create your own sense of the answer and whether it is True or False it will be the only answer that really works for you.

Perhaps the good news is that your fingers and eyes will have told you that this is a thin book. We have tried not to repeat the message and to differentiate between *Information* and *Communication*. In the world of work we classify *Communication* as the things that we *may need to know* where as *Information really matters to us*.

Lets consider an example, the company produced an in-house newsletter that communicated what was going on, one edition featured the employee team that had entered the marathon for a good charitable cause. This was a noble thing to celebrate, employees giving their time, energy, effort and crossing pain barriers for the benefit of others. In many sections of the company this text would have a positive effect on people's thinkboxes. However in other depots or divisions company employees did not receive the message in the context that it was presented. The in-house journal asked for comments on its overall content and the editorial team were surprised by one respondent, who said ' who cares who is running in the marathon? I would prefer to know what shift pattern I am working over the next few months, the effect that this answer will have on my earnings and the follow through into, can I pay my mortgage?' The employees in this part of the company needed Information messages to clear the confusions that impacted on their family and life, the in-house journal provided Communication messages that resulted in an Uh-Oh e-mail to the editors.

It's the context of the data exchange that creates the meaning, organisations need to ensure that most of the Information messages that define; what a good job is, let people know how they are doing in their work area, definitions of what the organisation expects and provides in return, these local messages must be understood, before the organisation can realise best value from the house journals. Apply the same argument in reverse and the positive. When individuals, teams and organisations have professional Information and Communication networks at local level, they will enjoy and value Corporate videos, telecasts and written communications on how the big world of their company is progressing. However if the local Information needs are not satisfied then you can expect Uh-Oh and confusion in the minds of the many as they make a personal, my Thinkbox judgement on what our corporation believes to be an important communication priority.

■ My necktop computer is scrambled - Uh-Oh!!

Your neck top computer is really smart and responds at *lightening* fast speed. Was there something wrong with lightening in the last sentence? No matter how quickly you read you will probably have registered lightning as the correct spelling of the word. Our thinkbox scanner detects things that are not right and sends us a 'we are not sure about this' signal. Something isn't right is accompanied by an uneasy body effect.

Mind and body are one - a confused Thinkbox always triggers a body effect. Simply said, Uh-Oh!! is the body effect that prepares us for the need to do something, react to the car horn, or prepare for that difficult message presentation to the Boss.

Uh-Oh!! is an impulse primer triggered by something in the top two inches of our body in the zone that we have christened - the Thinkbox.

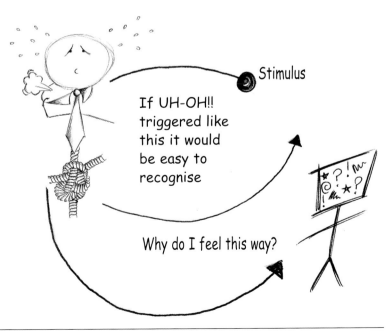

Stimulus

If UH-OH!! triggered like this it would be easy to recognise

Why do I feel this way?

When Uh-Oh arrives our Thinkbox and body move into automatic control mode – In an instant we experience the natural out of control, body and Thinkbox effects. This progression has two elements, a faster than we can think brain event and a tortoise trot body effect and fortunately we respond to the world at the speed of the lettuce eater. Our slow-go body mechanics create the time for us to think again before we react or respond.

One question that we routinely ask of our change programme delegates is - what is the body effect that you experience when you are under pressure? One delegate's heavily edited response was, "when I am under pressure - there is a part of my body, that usually follows the rest of my body, unless I am going to sit down, when it goes first- that twitches like a rabbits nose."

When you track the body effects of pressure at work you will realise that there are shallow and deep zones in this emotional pond. When you understand the body trigger that accompanies Uh-Oh do three things to break out of the rock logic control that your history prescribes as the way to respond.

First of all **Move** - change your bone, muscle and body set, relax your body

Then **Breathe deeply** - your breathing will have become shallow as your body works through Uh-Oh!!

Now **Look up** - you are now using new neural networks to analyse the Uh-Oh confusion.

Having taken these three simple steps you will be able to analyse the situation without the clutter of history. Your real time Thinkbox will now be able to deliver today's solutions to today issues and having modeled your Thinkbox for Change you will be better prepared for today's and tomorrow's challenges. Now you can respond instead of just reacting.

- Uh-Oh accompanies the need to stand up and do something

- First time karaoke performers wobble-old hands enjoy it

- Bruce Springsteen threw up before every performance

- Understand your body triggers

- Remember that Uh-Oh is the body's way of preparing you

- Uh Oh is the replay of old data stored on tablets of stone

- Sense Uh-Oh body changes, then move, breathe and look up

- Your real time thinkbox uses Pentium 49 processors, once engaged, they provide instant control

■ The shallow end of Uh-Oh

Print off this song sheet, perhaps changing the words to suit your work team. Then set the scene - you met a really good consultant at a monastery last weekend. She suggested that if each of us stands and sings this song to our colleagues - our world will change!

Here is the song that we want you to sing to the Live Aid theme tune.

> Feed the world make work a better place for you and for me and the entire human race.

> Uh - Oh - Uh - Oh you'll feel it, then hear it, and see it, its an Uh - Oh place with a different face.

> Feed your soul give it a respite place, for you and for you and the people in your space.

> Uh - Oh - Uh - Oh is going, when real time choices are flowing make work a better place for you and for me.

Brief your colleagues as follows. To make this an equal and fair process, under each of your chairs you will find a number, but don't look just yet. I want you to spend the next fifteen seconds analysing what your body is telling you right now. Then I'll announce the number under the chair that will determine who is going first.

Instruct the team to sense measure the experience and to register what they are thinking about you - their session leader - at this time. Explain that the consultant says it really doesn't matter if you talk-sing as opposed to real sing and that finger clicking and foot tapping are not allowed. She said we'll lose a higher level effect if we do this.

Now before I announce the running order, sense measure the whole body effect that you are experiencing. Pause, then announce - many of you will have moved out of your comfort zone and if you have you will now better understand the shallow end of Uh-Oh.

■ Leading is offering an opinion that others respond to

As the pace and extent of change in our world at work continues to accelerate we need to ensure that our Opinion Leaders at all levels in our organisations have the knowledge base and overall talent level that is equal to the challenge. When the organisations talent is equal to or greater than the challenge then results flow.

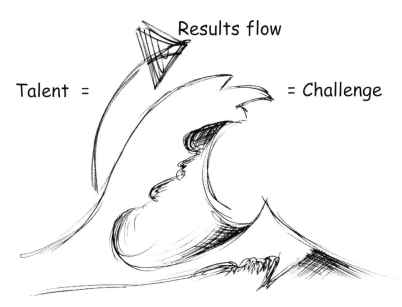

Results flow

Talent =   = Challenge

- **Change starts with me** has been at the core of New Era's change programme for a very long time. Real change in your organisation also starts with you, **when your world view changes**. Why will your world view change, how do you form new opinions? In our experience this happens in one of two ways, either your Thinkbox makes new connections and presents you with new ideas, or someone else does something or says something that makes a **difference to your Thinkbox.** Connecting with new ideas results in you seeing and describing and understanding things in a different way. New Thinkbox connections develop that make more sense to you, clarity in new thinking then replaces old confusions.

When you experience a period of hectic change your Thinkbox generates lots of ideas that just zoom around, with the prime objective of a new idea being to confuse the last idea that just whizzed away to somewhere. Now the middle of confusion can become a fertile time for an internal or external Thinkbox event or happening that joins up the dots. Considering the issues this way versus that way, usually results in clarity evolving from the dotty confusion, a new picture with dialogue and an - I'm Ok with this sense and feeling. The don't know loops seem to dissolve into a new solution and outcome, you now have a new Opinion on the issues. If you are first to the new ideas and communicate the thoughts in a way that connects with other people's thinkboxes, then you help others form new opinions too. You become an Opinion Leader, when people really listen to you and when you lead the teams thought process effectively.

Making sense of the situation and helping the people who work along side us design a Purpose is probably the most important aspect of work leadership that the Western world will face in the twenty first century.

The emerging industrial nations will have a similar effect in a labour cost context to that previously triggered by the coal, steel, oil and energy revolutions. The world map of where work will be done has already changed into a new dimension. Who will make sense of this for us? In many organisations the old ways of work, the comfortable work patterns, old agreements and the way we actually do our work will have to change, then change again, then change again. How do we form new Opinions that will lead to a Common Purpose amongst our working communities?

Professional Information and Communication networks, an understanding of where we are going and a joint perspective on how we will get there, in essence we need to rewire our Corporate brains for the issues of the future. We need to carry forward what currently works having benchmarked and tested its suitability for the future. In the Western world we have an enormous Thinkbox heritage embodied in our workforce. We need to harness and utilize this talent through an attitude shift geared to a Common Understanding and Purpose. The purpose is best captured as a simple statement that pops in everyone's Thinkbox and describes - **this is what we are trying to do, this is our Purpose.**

When we harness our Employee talent we have little to fear. We need to carry forward the best of the old way and think our way forward to address the issues of the future, we have trillions of megabite power in our Employee necktop computers just waiting to be switched on.

However if you ask a long stay opinion leader to think about a future that requires a change in the way they work - Uh-Oh is not too far away.

■ We were making steel when you were fighting Indians

We had organised a benchmark visit to a world class people plant in Logan Kentucky. If we return to an earlier Thinkbox message-you can only implement the world of work that you can describe- then visiting this plant fast tracks the description possibilities for everyone who visits, eventually that is. Changing our thinking doesn't come easy!! Most of our party were already switched on to the prospects of progressing their own organisations by following the new route map that our presenter was explaining. One of our party, a very experienced Operations man felt that he needed to ground and reality check these concepts by saying, ' this is all very well but what do you think that we can really learn from you boys - after all we were making steel when you boys were still fighting Indians'. Uh-Oh, everyone else in our party shrank at this completely out of context and insulting remark. Then our embarrassment deepened as the presenter in good American style explained that his forbears knew all about this. He explained that his lineage was twenty five percent Cherokee and xty percent Sioux- I really hoped that we were sitting on an ancient burial ground and that some higher force was going to open up the earth and let me disappear into it for a while.

Some hours passed and one of our party joked about Dinosaur Dan's quote of the week and as is often the case with humour the retelling of this story changed the pattern of our visit teams thinking. When embarrassment subsided (into a guessing game of what he might say or do next, and I will say we weren't disappointed) we realised that there was a vein of truth in the statement. In the following years as we gained a better understanding of high performance teams we found ourselves tracking back to the work practices of self directing teams in coal mines, pot banks, steel works, ship yards and the farming practices of the early to mid nineteen hundreds. Our

Grandads and Grandmas understood the essence of a work together community. Pride was communicated through very white smalls and a well washed front door step. Respect was handed down in well worn stories, "a hard days work for a hard days pay", "always do your best" and a whole litany of messages right the way back to three weeks entertainment for a ten bob note and life in a card board box int' middle of road.

Our thinkboxes are already programmed to do the right things, self organising, empowering, getting the job done together, we really didn't have too much to learn on the basics of how an organisation should operate effectively for the challenges of the twenty-first century. This visit was helping us understand that these principles were alive and really kicking in down town Kentucky when our organisations back home had forgotten about most of them. For us the organisational dots were joining up, we had a new sense of how this could work, we were describing something different, our opinions on the world of work were changing.

Perhaps the chunk down of the change process is from the organisations Thinkbox to group and team logics that then influence how individuals think and work. Are these the key to addressing the Change agenda for the future? Think back to the 'I don't care who is running in the marathon' story and remember that organisational change drives and survives on the Thinkbox perspectives of individuals, then group thinks, then department thinks that evolves into this is how our Organisation works.

In addressing the issues of change we need to better understand how our Thinkbox works, our necktop computer processes incoming data and creates our sense and meaning. We will explore how we deal with change at an individual level, then dip into group think and then on to the power brokers who form the Organisations Thinkbox through the rules and values that Employees experience through a work time within the organisation.

- Most employees can reflect on a period when work time went really well.

- As time passes we complicate simple work processes.

- Hands on and brains on work becomes over managed and over unioned as power plays complicate the work agenda.

- Change is a threat to power brokers.

- People defend their power base and lose track of the organisations purpose.

- Most employees know what they need to do.

■ Taking charge of change

For most of us change can be a bit of a shock. When something happens that affects our personal world, the force of this external power and how we deal with it, determines the short or long-term effect on the brain and body. Do we manage and work through such a change in a way that adds value to our experience or do we live on the receiving end of the natural tensions that accompany change in our personal world? Similarly when change occurs around us in our work place, if poorly managed or conducted the result can be a cumulative charge of employee energy that quickly evolves from confusion to resistance and then into low morale.

At work whenever the power base of even the smallest team is believed to be under threat, stand by for a realignment of power and a bumpy progression towards a new temporary stability. The Change effect is neither rational nor controllable, the outside influence - the change stimulus – needs only to become a reality in the mind of the people addressing the issues.

Within your organisation change triggers the maximum Uh-Oh!! effect for those who have power. The greater the power base, the bigger the threat to me, the more I stand to lose, then the deeper the heel marks in the sands of time as we prepare to resist. For Board members, Managers, Supervisors, Union Representatives or the informal power brokers - the Opinion Formers - within every team, the effects of change are the same and the outcomes are predictable.

Change for most of us is naturally problematic. Anything that disturbs our sedate and conventional life pattern releases the greatest electrical energy of all, brain waves. When the brain becomes excited then the Uh-Oh!! factor comes into play, as the Thinkbox channels the energy round and around the brain searching its data-base for an useful old connection that helps clear uncertainty.

Reacting to this disturbing, discomfort and resisting the change is a natural repetitive process that will continue to function until you rewire your Thinkbox to work in a different way.

There is at worst an equal amount of think energy required to resist change as is required to manage it. When confronted by a new circumstance our Thinkbox will search its data base and naturally choose the low resistance route, use old data networks, perhaps without consulting the person who should be driving the thinking bus, that is you.

Your world will become a better place when you understand the natural mechanics of the Thinkbox process, and learn how to channel Change-Think-Power into a learning and development loop. You can then become proactive in your approach to the change challenge and use this knowledge to help create better relationships and environment for people who live and work with you. When the Leaders of the power bases within an organisation understand themselves, they will be better able to harness the talent and think power of the people who work with and along side them.

Change starts with Me

Performance follows.

How does the Thinkbox work?

Goodness knows!! I look out of the aeroplane window as I write and travel over the fields and forests of Eastern Germany, my brain pops with thoughts about my Grand daughters, sons and with brain fast speed I visit my family on the ground and present and in the air of another place. Thinkbox energy pings around the brain visiting one hundred years of elapsed time history in seconds. Wonderfully out of control, you just have to follow where the brain takes you. I hope the computers and the pilots of the plane have more control over their technology and software systems than I do. Modern, computer controlled, fly by wire technology and an experienced flight crew with simple systems and structures will probably be able to help us all arrive on time at the right airport.

Whatever you do next - don't think of the colour orange. Quick wasn't it. Now think about oranges, did you get the smell and taste of an orange without asking? Recent studies on brain waves suggest that by the time that we consciously address an issue, our brain may be telling us the answer, before our real-time mind has considered the question. Our Thinkbox may assume that it needs to have worked out a response before they tune us in and perhaps risk us messing it up again. In spontaneous communication our Thinkboxes deliver prepared responses rich with the distillate of connected pictures, sounds and emotions.

When the brain is zapped with a high impact message from an external event or stimulus we sometimes take a hit-as Uh-Oh!! moves into control. Our Thinkbox needs time and context to cope with the effects of the impact and progress to a quiet mode before it can make sense of the incoming information and gradually move us to a considered evaluated response. If in the meantime we are getting excited, confused and flustered then the thinking part of our brain takes a timeout until our reaction subsides.

If left to its own devices your Thinkbox will respond to the stimulus and whizz you off into a lo resource state. But you have to pass through the body trigger spot as you follow the path to Uh-Oh.

When you are feeling down or under pressure analyse the part of your body that becomes tense. Is there anything that twitches like a rabbit's nose?

Confusion

Order

Messages can become confused when Uh-Oh strikes. We were at a sensitive stage in considering the future of a former Eastern German facility and on a plant tour we met the managing director who was showing another potential owner around. Uh-Oh manifests in a language triumvirate when the flusterer greeted us first in Russian, then with apologies in German before he eventually spoke in excellent English. The language that he would have chosen if he were driving the thinking bus.

Why was Herr Norrieger embarrassed? He was worried that he might be alienating his new owner by escorting the opposition. Why should this be an issue? The plant was insolvent and in this part of the new Germany they describe a good day as "I am alive and I have work". Our visit and that of the other possible owner could be helping secure work and this was a big issue for everyone. Herr Norrieger was trying too hard, he was afraid of failing.

An automatic response, driven by a fear of failing is the full orchestral equivalent of a karaoke moment. The higher the will to succeed or the need to deliver, then the deeper the immediate confusion that follows the brain's fast track analysis- I am going to fail-Uh Oh.

We didn't meet up with Herr Norrieger for the next few days, but we knew that the other potential owners had pulled out. You can guarantee that he had relived the Uh-Oh moment and built logics around what he should do, or say, when he met us next?

His thinkbox had been questioning itself. How had the encounter influenced our plans? Had he really blown it? What could he have done differently? We now know that he had created a mind monster and had fed the beast quiet a few buns before facts replaced assumptions and what ifs. When Uh-Oh kicks in we lose composure, focus, sleep and downtime control of what our thinkbox decides we are going to think about next.

Uh-Oh and confusion needs to give way to real time consideration of the facts, and this takes time.

■ Why do we know what we know?

When I gardened with my Grandad I learned that wireworms need to be killed at both ends, otherwise the tail will grow a head and the head will grow a tail. Of course this is true, everything my Grandad said was true and my Grand daughters who garden with me will need to understand this fact of gardening life. However the intervening years and life styles require a different despatch method, topping and tailing may not appeal to two young vegetarians. Wireworm swimming lessons in the same pond as the hungry tadpoles serves the same purpose. One hundred years of knowledge transferred in the telling and now installed in a new young Thinkbox. Much of what we know is handed down from the people who raised us and the stories we re-tell are part of our Thinkbox memory bank. What other information do we retain and how do we access the stored data?

Sit down in a quiet place. Ask your mind to take you back to the earliest class or schoolroom that you can remember. What do you recall and where does your brain take you next? Sights, sounds, smells and even the emotions associated with the memory. If your mind tracked to  a good memory you can enjoy the play back and revisit the emotions associated with the time that you revisited.

A not so pleasant memory could equally be the outcome of the classroom recall. I was one of the jokers in the class, our history master had a lifeless lower arm, very useful as a gadget wielded from behind to the back of the head of distracting pupils. Forty years on how can I revisit my dazed state and capture other aspects of the classroom and fellow pupil information with ease.

How can I recall this information today and readily describe so accurately through a connect with the past? Our mid-brain stores information and relays and replays when we explore the Thinkbox archives.

Who knows what the long-term effects of Thinkbox-bashing by a paralysed arm will be? Perhaps my three-sector brain has merged slightly more than yours, undamaged brains operate via three networked sections, the inner, the outer and the mid-brain.

The Three Part Brain

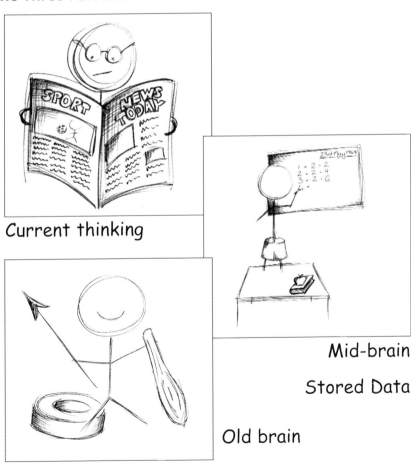

Current thinking

Mid-brain

Stored Data

Old brain

■ Managing your Thinkbox.

As soon as you start to understand some of the mechanics of your box, managing 'you' becomes a little easier. Understanding the archived data in the mid-brain-works is fairly simple. What went in as stored data is what comes out. In response to a today stimulus the mid-brain replays the whole suite of memory information. Ask your Thinkbox to take you back to your early years. Think Grandma or some other oldie - where did the Thinkbox take you via an audio-visual reality tour with senses and emotions restored. Whilst the smell of bread may be my stimulus the picture image of the open kitchen fire with an old smoke heritage fills my nostrils. Warm lovely memories forever.

This is all fine and well with the good times. The fact that whatever we experienced on the good side of life will replay on request is a blessing. But what about the bad memories, they return with the full suite of emotions as well. In living our lives today we can be limited by our past experience and not enjoy life to the full. Fortunately for us, as well as the midbrain mechanics we have an outer brain and by using this part of the Thinkbox we can easily detach from our midbrain history. If you revisit an old memory or event that disturbs you today you can use the outer brain to change and update the data.

Quietly analyse the smells, sounds, sights and emotions associated with the memory, then change some of the mechanics of the data. In your mind replace a coloured image with black and white, change a movie to a still, capture the image and move it further away as if you were defocusing with a telescope. When you change the mechanics of the memory using your outer brain, you replace old data with new data. The pictures and sounds associated with the memory may not be the cause of your concerns it's probably the associated emotions that disturb you today. Changing the characteristics of the memory automatically disengages the old feelings and emotions. Without this change then it's baggage in and the same baggage out. Information on NLP [Neuro Linguistic Programming] via an e-mail search or from your library will provide more of the tools and techniques that you will need, but please register these words right now - **only you can change the data - when you do change the data in real time today you lose the old connections and associated emotions.** In summary our mind store challenge to you, is to enjoy the good and revisit the not so good. Use the outer brain to engage with and enjoy the stored information.

- How does the outer brain connect with the inner?

What is controlling your breathing right now? You will already have taken a deeper breath as your real time outer brain decides to check that you are. As your conscious mind concentrates on other things, body function controls become the domain of our inner brain, life drivers operate without us needing to think or worry about them.

■ Thinkbox past and present

In a thinking context the concept of inherited memories is becoming more and more important. What memory networks have been passed down from the history of our relations, is there a connect with all of our family who have walked this earth before us? How much of the way we are is predetermined? To what extent are we captive to the brain data of history?

In the same way as our physical and attitudinal style relates to our parents and grandparents so does our memory bank. The natural skills of oratory or sport, the way we stand or walk and talk can be part of a gene bank easily connected to other people from the same historic network. For good or for better we are who we are and we know that most of our responses are programmed and stored. Hunger, the need for a drink or a cigarette; the body's reactions to demanding exercise follow a predictable automatic patterned response. How does your body tell you that you need a coffee or a window open? Mind and body are one and there is a body effect signal that starts us thinking about what next. Similarly, when we move out of our comfort zone old historic networks signal a Thinkbox connection to a body effect.

From the mid-brain, used data can be recalled in the same context as it was stored. From the old brain [that is the inner brain] programmed responses with chemical support provide the automatic fix prescribed by our ancestors and handed down in the same way as they handed down eye colour. In response to a stimulus, the old brain automatically injects adrenaline and we run!! The same way as we always did. A different stimulus and this time the old brain sprays us with neo adrenaline, with this fix, we fight, every one of us, born with the hard wired neural chemistry and mechanics of flight or fight. If the old brain delivers adrenaline you either respond to the fix and run or understand that this Uh-Oh!! signal will go away - if the old brain delivers its second favourite cocktail a Neo-fix you are prep'd for a fight, again only a real-time-outer brain thinking response to Uh-Oh!! can produce another reaction. You will need to interrupt the automatic stimulus –response cycle and deal with the information within your current awareness to produce a different outcome to the natural one.

- They used to say 'pressure creates character'.

- Oh no it doesn't, your history, geneology and experience have already done this.

- Moving out of your comfort zone - into Uh-Oh - opens up powerful old brain networks.

- Uh-Oh is junkie land.

- Move, breathe and look up - this is the in-control path through this event.

- Only fix free Thinkboxes can function with composure.

- Old brain and mid brain process old data.

- Today belongs to you-make the best of it.

How old is thinkbox past?

Meme logic is in vogue right now with the usual new wave enthusiasm. Research, study conferences and perhaps an over complication of our basic Thinkbox characteristics. Memory data handed down in the same way as Genes equals Memes. But why not, if you have your mother's eye colour and in later life her arthritis all from the family gene bank, then why should our Thinkbox inheritance be significantly different. Arguably we are born with our parental brain software that will condition our early life responses. However we will not leave this world with the Thinkbox we arrived with, life experience will rewire in line with what works and leave us to manage Uh-Oh!! when the developing Thinkbox system makes the wrong judgement calls.

Life conditioning starts with the people who created us followed by the people who brought us up. Early patterns of what is OK and Not OK are sponsored by those around us and on life's bumps and bruises we very often learn the hard way. Learning is rarely a straight line progression to staying out of harms way for one simple reason. Our thinkboxes **don't understand don't**. Please don't touch your big sister's new fragile doll results in a careful appraisal of who is around or watching and then a very determined touch. Similarly **don't you dare** give Granddad a really really big hug, always works. What we say and in a Thinkbox context the message we convey can lead to two very different outcomes.

Fast forward life's learning curve by twenty years and apply the same theory. 'I don't want you to interpret this communication as a white wash job' equals ' he is going to cover things up again. Whenever we are told what **not to think** our Thinkbox data-processing capability is so quick that Oops its too late. Our listeners will automatically tune into the words that align with their own interpretation of the message – **don't think about** becomes **think about** with **don't trust the messenger** as the automatic and predictable outcome.

When we enter the world of work the way we are as programmed by parenting, school, education and broad life experience becomes the base line for the next phase of our development. New rules, the need to adapt and fit in, the formulae for doing well, all provide a Thinkbox and developmental challenge. Memes - the messages from history, are much more powerful in an organisational context than as long stay drivers on personal thinking. Your work place has a Thinkbox of its own, collective thoughts and memories of what worked and what didn't work evolve into the do's and don'ts of your working life.

Within your organisation the stories and lessons of history are maintained by a series of gate keepers who use their power to make sure that things are done in the right way. Very powerful - this is how it is and this is how we do things around here have accumulated over time.

Just imagine that when you look at the string of Accountants in the canteen queue that just behind the most powerful lady in that line there is a small holy cow on a string carrying the corporate tablets of stone, labeled bean counting in OurDotcom. Behind the long stay manager who happens to be the local expert on aircraft safety, eight yaks and a sherpa carrying fifteen updates of the Civil Aviation regulations and with the Senior Trade Union steward five possible interpretations of everything that has been written on most things. Walking, talking, Thinkbox archives, with an instant you can't do this or that bibliography. You might even be shown the original tablets of stone if you stay around long enough. With each new job comes a honeymoon period and how long you stay in your comfort zone may be determined by the time it takes for you to cross one of the big power brokers, irrespective of tribe. Old tribes are a good analogy here as many of the powerbrokers in established business really do operate with Directorsaurus or Brotherex logics fashioned to protect their personal power base and hopefully the best interests of their specific tribes. When Directosaurus meets Brotherex with attendant tribes you can sometimes sense the jungle from the atmosphere in the room.

Rock logics, tablets of stone that were appropriate in times gone by very often become the epitaphs for failed businesses. Ironically it's the new kids on the block and perhaps the informed outsiders who are probably better equipped to distinguish the useful from the old and the path that will help organisations survive. By balancing the strengths from the old way with the requirements of the future, organisations can change the way that they work.

The new kid on the block effect associated with a new comer to an organisation always triggers Uh-Oh. And if it's a senior player with power the whole organisation wobbles. One of our associates was head hunted to advance the supply chain thinking by thirty years in a long established Marks & Spencer supplier. She was an expert on Thinkboxing and change and knew what to expect, but looked forward to learning more through this new company experience. Having been recruited by the executive board into a high profile role, relationships were professional but guarded with the senior production leaders who had long term working relationships with middle and junior managers. Within days of arriving the organisation communicated its thinking towards the new employee in what borders on a series of almost spiritual events. At first strange things were happening at night and eventually in broad daylight. Desk equipment moved, files couldn't be found, misleading data was presented and most obvious of all – her chair moved.

Leaving the open plan office for even ten minutes she returned to colleagues who were apparently hypnotised into motionless gazes at their computer screens and to the mystery of the missing chair – mind game on!!

Move, breathe, look up, walk the length of the open office and push a chair from the conference room to the workstation all in full view of her senior production colleague's window.

There were a whole series of tests and trials that new-kids-on-the-block have to pass to join the tribe. When you understand that these strange behaviours are really an expression of passion and pride in the 'old way'. And that you need to move the organisations comfort blanket with many hands as well as yours to integrate new ideas into the old ones.

There is always a time lag on the journey to working in a new way. The new kid's ideas can only be grafted on with the blessing of the power brokers. You have to pass the tests, but you should draw the psychological line for your colleagues well before they ask you to kill a lion.

Now with all of this historic drag how can we develop a momentum for change? The prime mover for progressive change is usually a **thinking shift** supported by a Power base and perhaps an overall alignment with the following equation.

Right ideas x Right time x Powerful voice = Success

When you review the death dance of an old organisation you will find that too much resource and time and energy was wasted by the powerbrokers, posturing over rock logic recall and responses with past experience and positioning a guaranteed failure path to tomorrows agenda. Dinosaurs enjoy recalling and living yesterday's battles whilst they make low deep growling noises to persuade their own tribe that they have the answer.

Old ideas x Three years too late x Conflicting voices = Memeland

You didn't join this organisation with an expectation of it failing did you? All your effort, hard work and commitment is willingly given to deliver a result for you and your business. Didn't those years at work go quickly and what were you able to do to help influence your work colleagues and perhaps your organisation's thinking on the best way forward. At work we learn and grow into the organisation in a similar way to our early learning life experience, that is from the people that we interact with and perhaps look up to.

Our Thinkbox learns best through models, and role models form an important part of our thinking development. The whole organisation 'boss watches' we automatically appraise bosses or colleagues leadership style and in the search for what works you can fast track some to-do's and sometimes learn the not–to-do's. An old boss of mine had moved to a senior position in our company. He had a quick temper and associated fuse, his impressions of Mr Angry when we failed to deliver the Plan were known company wide and this worked for him. We were similar people types products of the same environment, but what worked for him didn't work for me.

Recognising that the automatic response of the jungle fighter to a challenge wasn't working was the first step in reprogramming my responses to one better suited to my work environment and the development of a leadership behaviour that worked. What is the best process to use en-route to behaving in a new way? Firstly recognise the disconnect between today's world and the old behaviour, then rewire for a new response installing an agro-circuit-breaker en route to a diplomat's button. Now instead of blowing a fuse in an historic, rock logic, predictable, stone-age response mechanism that occurs naturally, direct the same impulse energy down a different path. Rewire for the appropriate response for working life in the twenty first Century. Jungle fighter - meet the Diplomat. Gradually open up a new energy track that activates when Uh-Oh!! tells you that you need to do something. You can configure a new way of responding, where you think through an outcome rather than using nature's way that didn't deliver the result the last time. The intervention process and the subsequent Thinkbox rewiring prepares us to engage the outer brain. Now remember only quiet brains work within the context of considered responses. Inner-old brain and the recorded messages from the mid-brain can only deliver pre-programmed responses based on old data, all the way back to me Jane, you can swing on that old creeper if you like!!

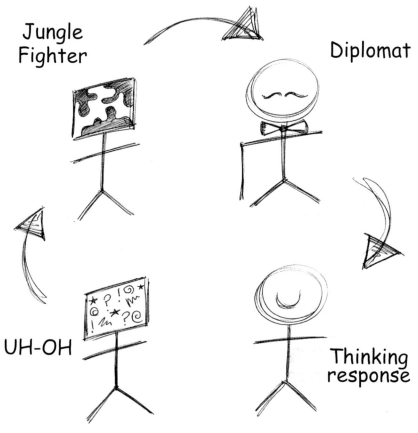

Jungle
Fighter

Diplomat

UH-OH

Thinking
response

When we are in control, capable and operating with steady state issues the calmness and peace is embracing, Thinkbox in neutral, all is well. In a similar but opposite response when the old brain triggers Uh-Oh!! and orders a fight, the real time Thinkbox stays in neutral as you metaphorically strangle the person who has just cut you up on the motorway. Did you plan to speed to 90mph to block them in, was it a thoughtful considered response? Or did the neural networks of Uh-Oh!! automatically determine what next.

Old and mid-brain are wired with powerful energy tracks and to move from predictable response to considered action we need to understand the physics of our Thinkbox circuits and resultant body effects. Fortunately mind and body operate as one. We can use the comparatively slow response time of senses, muscles and bones, then with the ability to recognizing the early physical side of Uh-Oh!! we have time to develop a considered and appropriate response versus an automatic one.

- Our family's history conditions our early development

- Your thinkbox doesn't do "Don't"

- Organisations develop a thinkbox via experiences

- Power broker messages condition the world of work

- Honour history but let go of old logics

- Give the diplomat the key, to let the jungle fighter out of its box

■ Your organisation has tribe logics at all levels.

■ The interpretations of what's true change as you move from tepee to tepee.

■ You will find that the night shifts collective brain is programmed in a different way to the day shift.

■ The head office tribes rarely connect with the logics of outlying settlements.

■ Union and management tribes have a very catholic decision making process - wait until you see white smoke from the tepee.

■ Old and ancient orders can only change very slooooowly.

Please leave organisational Memeland for now and return to the loops and logic of how your personal Thinkbox works. We will return to the organisational context later and explore the games that dinosaurs play, but first lets explore some more on how you can make a difference.

Hi

Comfort Zone opens when the Talent is equal to the Challenge

Happy Bunny curve

First and foremost let's begin by understanding the mind and body effect of life on the Hi side, the in-control-mode. You are physically relaxed, breathing moderate to slow and probably deeply, you have clear focus on what next and a composure that provides inner confidence. This is the quiet brain mode, there is a natural order at work, you are feeling good. Yes!! let's start the day, something orders the body to skip and it does in an easy and satisfying way. When challenged you respond like a racehorse destined to win, one swish of the whip, acceleration when required, with a sustainable difference over the opposition. Work challenge or pressure situation, just increase the pace, you are performing within your capability zone, and your talent is equal to or greater than the challenge. At the end you will reflect on a good day. How does this work? We could do with the same formula tomorrow!!

Analyse the component parts of a controlled you. Understand the body effect that associates with success. You may not find this an easy thing to do on it's own, but by contrasting the difference between the resourceful in-control state when you are on a Hi with the Uh-

Oh!! perspective of out of-control, you can easily calibrate and recognise the in-control characteristics and components. Think measure your emotions - if in control relaxed and capable is a ten, is my current Uh-Oh!! confusion and discomfort a level three or four? By contrasting the difference you can clearly calibrate yourself to understand the eight to ten zone within which you are resourceful, capable and relaxed, you are a happy bunny!!.

Your eight to ten zone experience is easily captured, it's called a good day. An OK time window when you enjoyed the world and its people. Now move a little deeper into your Happy Bunny zone, you need to understand your muscle set and breathing rate. Capture and sense measure the dimensions of a great drive down the fairway or a really meaningful interaction with a person or a team. Work at designing and understanding the logic bubble that captures the in control and capable you and develop the skill of calling up this new meaning configuration in your head. Describe it in words and in body speak, label this the Hi resource state. Work at this until you can almost hold the description out in front of your head and look at it, replay with words and resense the wholesome memory. This is the OK today process. Capture the moment, fully sensed into one soap bubble. Recall it when you need it.

Capturing and recalling the components of Hi is a very important part of being able to contrast the difference between Hi and Uh-Oh, the Lo. When calibrated by body zone the early warning signs of moving towards a bad day can be sensed through a body effect and changed. Uh-Oh!! is an old brain and old data process, it's the Thinkbox way of telling us to prepare, something is about to or Oops is already happening. Uh-Oh!! is your body's bugle call to a challenge – summoning resources – and forewarning there is a change on the way!!

Have you heard a bump in the night- waking to thoughts of what was that noise? Did I lock the car? Is someone removing the new lawn mower from the garage? Is our television walking out of the door?

More listening and noise equals there is someone there, as you walk around the darkened house, bump, bump,bump, your whole being stops as you ask yourself- what was that noise? Relax - its only your heart beating and you are already prepared for the intruder - Uh-Oh!! with associated chemistry makes sure that you are. Meoww-I'll strangle that cat, sleep usually returns slowly.

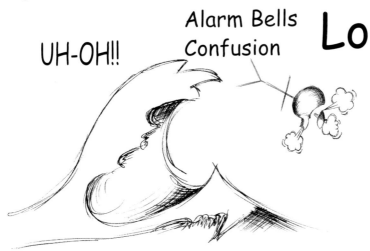

Alarm Bells

UH-OH!!   **Confusion   Lo**

Ask a person who dislikes wobbles and heights to climb a ladder. Sweaty palms and maybe arms, shallow breathing, tensed muscles and general confusion are the characteristics of Uh-Oh!! and out of control. Did the reluctant ladder climber decide to tense their muscles, move to a shallow breathing pattern, pressurise internally to increase both pulse and blood pressure!! Old and mid -brain combine in subconscious control to constrain and confuse. Anyone in this condition understands both Uh-Oh!! and out of control. Gone is the comfort zone and in its place a debilitating energy sapping life condition formulated on old data and associated fear and response programmes. Heights can produce Uh-Oh!! for some of us whilst confined space or the rat or spider can produce a similar effect in others. Whilst the trigger for Uh-Oh!! will be different the mechanics of moving out of control are the same for all of us.

When whatever it takes to move us out of our comfort zone occurs we either manage and tame Uh-Oh!! or we live with it.

However, between Thinkbox stimulus and action we have an elastic time window. The decision process of - what do I do or say now when fore warned by Uh-Oh!! opens an useful time capsule. **When Uh-Oh!! strikes do nothing except think it through.** Register and associate the body signals that accompany the start of Uh-Oh!! then progressively hard wire a new thinking control loop. Your Thinkbox works so quickly that we can programme considered and evaluated response versus natural reaction and no one but you needs to know.

Think about chocolate.

Now did that hurt? Uh-Oh will only arrive for the professional diet person when they think about chocolate. For the rest of us it is an OK thought and effect. When you deliberately and slowly think about your favourite food, does your mouth start to salivate? Stimulus from the text on this paper drives a sense-associated response, thought stimulated body effects that are OK and easy to live with. Now think on, to the music from the Jaws movie, visualise the shark surfacing in a blood stained sea or some other Uh-Oh!! video or televised experience.

Analyse the difference between a "Chocolate" response and Uh-Oh!! Compare steady state, comfortable and O.K., with a fear or other sense based emotional hit. At the shallow end of the emotional pond understand the body effect of watching the winner on the podium, hearing the anthem and then move to the deeper waters by remembering a loved family member who is now in the other place. Now step out of that brain web and ask yourself, **what is an emotion? It is only a played back memory with a feeling attached**. To our benefit or pain, emotions are feeling laden thoughts with old data incorporated.

Emotion is just an old thought with an old feeling attached

Muscles usually tense

You can choose to spend most of your time in the 'in control - considered response' mode or you could decide to stay in the automatic Uh-Oh zone. Both become a clear cut choice option for all of us. With a simple methodology you can move from an emotional and perhaps limiting automatic response to a considered, controlled, interaction. Firstly calibrate your Thinkbox to recognize the physical symptoms of Uh-Oh!! Stomach tightening, general muscle fix, a heat effect in our palms, under arms or a flush effect throughout the body but common to all a general sense of out of control and confusion.

This body effect communicates that Uh-Oh has already arrived. The old brain has administered the appropriate dosage of get ready drugs and you will not be fit to drive the thinking bus until the fix wears off. When Uh-Oh!! hits use these three steps to regain thinking composure **Pause before responding**, let the chemical brain douche subside enabling a fix-free response. **Greet Uh-Oh!!** by redirecting the energy away from the **automatic response circuit** to a - **Why do I feel this way** network? Using this process your outer brain moves into control, you are now in thinking charge and can make a better, more thoughtful decision on how you respond.

Out of Control loop

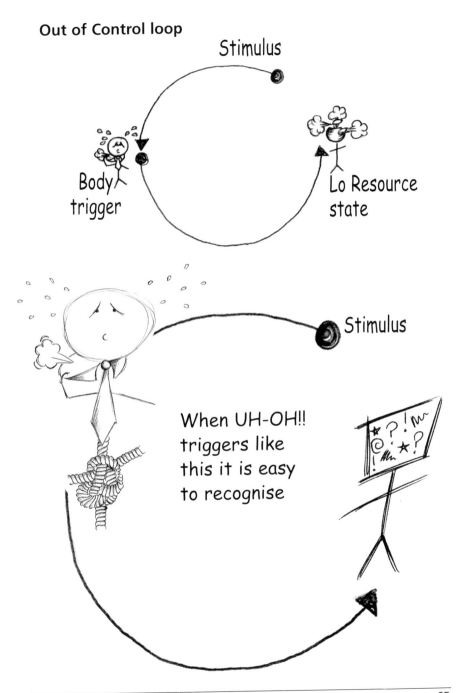

Stimulus

Body trigger

Lo Resource state

Stimulus

When UH-OH!! triggers like this it is easy to recognise

■ Happy or sad emotions that you experience today are a replay of old Thinkbox data.

■ Mind and body effects combine into a now experience.

■ The powerful old brain activates chemical and physical changes much quicker than you can comprehend.

■ The way you react drives from old data. Instinctive, repetitive, rock like logics.

■ Body trigger sensing creates awareness.

■ Ask why do I feel this way?

■ Now you drive the thinking bus.

Your Thinkbox automatically generates confusion with associated muscle and bone changes when Uh-Oh strikes. When you register the physics of the change ask yourself one question -

Why do I feel this way? W.D.I.F.T.W.

This question moves the decision making to your real time, today, thinkbox allowing you to make informed decisions, as opposed to the old emotion laden alternative. You will have disengaged from the old data networks and from history.

Body Trigger → Pause → Move → Breathe, Look up → Considered Response

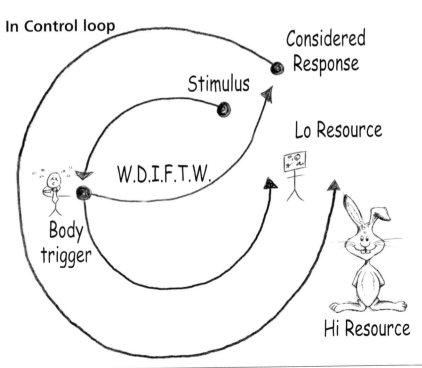

You now have a new Thinkbox control network. With experience and practice it will help you accommodate increasingly powerful electrical brain streams through a dissipative control loop. Like the church on a hill in an electrical storm, outstandingly tall almost encouraging the strike. When lightning hits, the energy is directed and earthed with no great effect. You can develop emotional energy networks that help you stand tall when the emotions of your team or environment become charged. **This is real leadership, when someone makes sense of a situation and helps clear other people's confusion - They lead the team's thinking.** To conduct the energy you just need to understand what is going on and apply some simple basics that help You-steer-You through the stormy action.

Remember only quiet brains can think clearly, Uh-Oh!! is an old brain automatic response combined with a mid-brain search for an appropriate experience connection. There is a real time Thinkbox alternative to your natural reaction to Uh-Oh!! Understanding how Uh-Oh!! develops its energy is an important first step towards a solution. When Uh-Oh arrives ask it to explain itself!!

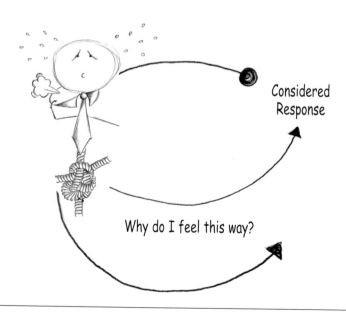

Considered
Response

Why do I feel this way?

■ Uh-Oh!! naturally triggers a Thinkbox search

What does it take to move us into a confused and out-of control mode, what event or Thinkbox message moves us out of our comfort zone the quickest? As you analyse the triggers of the Uh-Oh!! effect you may replay the same old internal messages, a voice in your head or perhaps a combination of voice and pictures pops up from the archives. **These messages may ping you at three a.m.** as the Thinkbox works on the data and explores old and mid-brain connections. At the end of your Thinkbox search for a reason for Uh-Oh!!, the analysis may point in the direction of one of the following;

- Fear of failure
- Letting someone down
- Losing face or grace or anything that is important to you
- Not meeting a loved ones expectations
- Not meeting your own expectations
- Unfair treatment in working and family life - this is a biggy!!
- Or at the shallow end, not completing your list

These will be at the top of most peoples Uh-Oh!! cycle, are they close to yours?

Most of these factors and others will generate brain wave energy, body effects and confusion from old data and well-programmed response networks. If one of the above connects today, you will automatically suffer the same body effect that greeted the same circumstances yesterday or even last year. For example-the more important your drive to achieve results-the greater the negative energy that you need to conduct when results are illusive. If the real reason that you can't deliver is someone else's poor performance then Uh-Oh!! rarely encourages the best of behaviours. You will probably need to reintroduce the Jungle fighter to the Diplomat. However if you don't rewire your Thinkbox circuits your brain will continue to use the old networks. Historic data and events then impact on today's emotional states.

This bunny has overdosed on old data

One of my Grandad 's messages was **'always do your best'**. Don't be surprised if you find your behaviour today is directly related to a very old message. The more deep rooted the message the greater the associated Uh-Oh!! When the message pops it doesn't arrive alone, with Grandad's words I am transported to a house then a green house and a garden or a shed with smells and I'll stop now before I run out of paper. When a work colleague or situation dictates that you cannot perform **to your best** they need to realise that they may be tangling with your Grandad as well as with you - Internal voice says 'always do your best' Uh Oh!! when you don't, is then automatic.

■ Given a challenge - it is in the nature of woman to work at it until it is achieved

Experience is not about what happens to you. It's about how you deal with what happens to you. If the first few efforts at resolving Thinkbox challenges fail then at least you have learned not to use the same process again. Only when you repeat the failures should you be hard on yourself. When something that you do is not working, doing something different often leads to a successful outcome. But we do need to train the brain to cope with Uh-Oh!! Fitness coach messages 'there is no gain without pain' - is equally relevant to our brain.

Let's explore the links-five minutes on the treadmill at seven km per hour will be easier tomorrow than it was today. As your body fitness progresses by this time next week you will need to spend fifteen minutes to achieve the same workout effect. Now for legs and lungs substitute Thinkbox components. When you work under pressure you adapt to the mental strains, the biggies like cynicism and sneyd remarks are taken within in your stride, thus extending the composure capacity of the Thinkbox. Use the enormous computing power of the Thinkbox to psyche yourself to new performance levels - big issues Thinkbox reduced to their real size.

■ Re-directing the attack energy

My niece, who is pretty, talented, very creative and fun, used to be thin. The only broad thing she possessed was a smile. For some reason or another, but probably boyfriend related-she took up kickboxing. "Rachel has started kickboxing", if she kicks anything, something will break and if anyone kicks her Uh-Oh!! lets call the ambulance now!! In the same way that Rachel has become skilled through practice at surviving a heavy foot onslaught by deflecting the force. Practice can develop Thinkbox response power and confidence in your ability to cope with the mental and emotional thwacks to the head that your world aims in your direction. Thinkboxing is the mental equivalent of the other forms of martial arts. You can marshal your mental resources to help you stay in control as well as managing the physical effects of being on the receiving end of a Thinkbox thwack.

Simply re-direct the incoming energy, don't take the hit to heart. Track Uh-Oh!! into real time thinking and simply re-direct the Thinkbox energy in the same way as a kick boxer does the physical force.

When you understand your body trigger and can interpret your resource state you can translate **Uh!Oh!! to - "What can I learn from this"?** Having programmed the response network, you will be better prepared for the unexpected.

Pressure pot   Happy Bunny

Think model a problematic experience and then hard wire through the developing knowledge of what will work to resolve the problem using considered thought. Develop your ideas from theory and test the ideas through practice, acknowledge what works and agree not to repeat what didn't work. For example the start point for a constructive response to pressure is your belief logic. Incorporate one powerful circuit breaker into your control network. **Confidence in You - press your self-esteem button every time that Uh-Oh!! hits**, believe you can resolve the issue and you are best placed to deal with the problem. First register the body response, let the excited brain bubble down, and analyse the issue with real time non emotional data. Burst the emotional balloon, recognise and absorb the Uh-Oh!! effect, pause-then analyse. Remember the rock logic network buster.

Move → Breathe → Look up

Through your growing understanding of an in-control and capable you, you also develop the ability to help others. Let other people's attack become part of your Thinkbox-defence. Your most passionate opponents can be disarmed when you manage their attack energy with understanding and help them move towards better solutions. Through practice you can help them towards outer brain thinking solutions. Given a problematic attack message, ask them to tell you *More*, understand then *Explore*, peel the emotional onion until you get to the **Crux**, were you expecting **Core?** That's rock logic I'm afraid, predictable automatic connect-works!!

Angry   Wise

When someone is out of control they are probably driven by rock logic too, fixed, predictable, knee jerk, self-preserving reaction to a problem situation using old data and behaviour patterns. Now how do you move this situation to a Mrs Angry personal insight of – 'I'm probably in attack mode for reasons I don't fully understand'. Or I always react this way when I'm confused. Think it through from their perspective, calmly and from a detached-emotions-in-control-world-view. Think-If I can reframe this troublesome energy, I know I can help this lady make a better contribution. Your own beliefs and expectations are the first filter on the interaction. If you are expecting an irrational bonehead, you will see and hear one-this is guaranteed. Nothing is surer, in the people and relationships business, you will get what you expect, so programme yourself to expect the best from people. Set aside your reactionary thoughts and find out what they think and perhaps why, understand what is driving their bus. Mrs Angry behaves that way for a genuine reason, with its origins deep in the Thinkbox.

Having developed a belief in the underlying O.K-ness of people you can swallow your reaction to a You-are-Not-O.K message and better digest the initial Uh-Oh!! situational challenge. Automatically engage your thinking brain, short circuit your old emotional response networks and deploy real time thinkpower resources to resolve the issues. The next step is to link back to what is important in this interaction between two people, reframe to a bigger picture and consider this interaction from that perspective.

When a good working environment with an honest process for resolving real differences between people is what is really important to you, then most of the Uh-Oh!! managing network is already in place and prepared. You now use this Thinkbox process to help you-control-you through the interaction.

When your **Thinkbox is programmed to add value** you will increase its potential and capability every time you use it in this way. As the thinking apprentice that you will inevitably be in the early stages of development, your circuits will sometimes fuse into confusion, similar to your house wiring when a bulb overheats and the power cuts off through the circuit breaker. But as you work through the confusion process your Thinkbox learns. Having resolved low order personal confusion issues today managing similar low order issues becomes easy and automatic. You then progressively upgrade your capability and each time you overcome a higher level challenge you increase your ability to manage your reaction to change.

- Asking your Thinkbox to - 'just wait a few milliseconds' creates space for today thinks.

- Responding to your body trigger and asking Uh-Oh to explain itself is a powerful disconnect with old data.

- With practice your Thinkbox can be programmed to focus on new solutions through new networks.

- Belief in your ability to manage really difficult challenges will grow through practice and experience of what works.

- When the going gets tough, default to added value exchanges.

■ Thinkbox Games Organisations Play

Corporate Uh Oh!! comes into play when an event or action takes the combined think power of many brains out of our work related comfort zone. When Uh-Oh!! triggers the people groups who work with us often respond in predictable ways. If they do that, we hit Uh Oh!!, so we do this, a time honoured cause-effect-reaction loop is established. Organisations can work to a **"you do–we do-script"**. For example you reduce overtime, we slow the work down, to create overtime. Whilst the behaviour that we are going to explore has a dramatic context it is best described as a Game. Expressed simply a game is a repetitive behaviour that the Thinkbox tracks to when required. The purpose of the little drama is to repeat the effect that the game achieved when last played. The key difference between a game and other interactions is that when an organisation is in game mode the communications have a hidden agenda.

Use the management team briefing as an example. Contrast the words used with the meanings exchanged. The senior manager briefs the Employees and says , "We need to reduce our cost base." Mr Angry explodes and repeats the message that won applause in the last meeting when costs were discussed. This message can be seven years old and the game may have been played out with three previous managers.

Think of the script for the drama as written in stone or at least rock logic. The manager says, "Cost down" workforce thinks "Is this management speak for overtime cuts - or job losses?" Mr Angry presses the reaction button and Uproar follows. When overtime is threatened the workforce usually roll out temp labour or contractors and build a rock logic - agreement - restrictive practice castle to protect their earnings. Safety issues and a rash of grievances usually compound the confusion.

The depth of passion in this type of interaction is normally driven by individuals emotional reactions. Passionate people pop up and tell their tales. Mr. Angry has at least five back up war stories to add to his initial message, right the way through to the contractor drove a Rolls Royce. His wisdom has been brewed in an oak cask and you may be dealing with a ten-year-old blend of rumour, fact, supposition, and discussion all exaggerated into a super story. It works like this.

Every time you discuss cost down in employee meetings Mr. Angry says exactly the same thing. Uproar-follows!! what about this cost, that cost and anything get's airtime except what about my cost. Questions, like "Am I taking more out of this business than I have rightly earned", rarely surface in the discussion. He is very often repeating exactly the same mess-room story that he knows will be supported by other employees. Mr Angry probably isn't the author, some one else wrote the script then the high airtime joker or the drama king in the team acts out the scenario - again.

Games are pre-programmed scripts normally conjured up to protect something that the player has and is afraid of losing. The more significant the possible loss the greater the intensity of the drama that will be played out.

The passionate people in your organisation operate as opinion pods, with two factions. The really bright or informed thinkers, usually long stay employees, that people turn to for help and ideas - Opinion formers. Then you have their close cousins the idea pushers - High air time, eloquent with a need to dominate sometimes to the point of bullying.

Idea pushers who operate in the open are manageable, when they operate in a more covert way the organisation's life becomes complicated.

Managers often force feed their teams with dodgy ideas too, under the cover of power and threats.

When the leaders at all levels in the organisation are in Uh-Oh - game playing is a likely outcome.

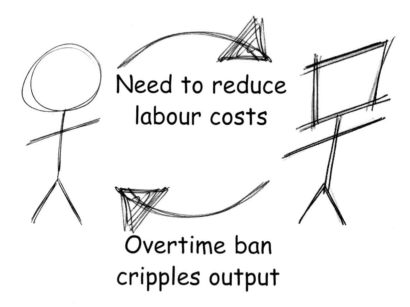

Need to reduce
labour costs

Overtime ban
cripples output

■ NjNj - The Niggle Joke Game

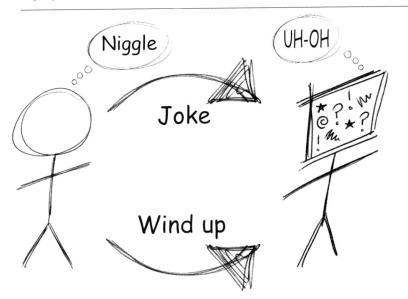

Humour can be used as part of a scripted outcome Game and is normally a feature in most people and groups communication agenda. Jokes involve a clever Thinkbox trick that Game players use to their advantage. The storyteller feeds you some words, you then develop a story line in your mind, thinking ahead of the story teller - your Thinkbox works twice as fast as the voice box can send the words, we transmit at about 250 words per minute, and think at close to 450 wpm. As the story unfolds it takes a completely different direction to the one that you had preformed in your mind and you laugh at how stupid you were. Does that make sense, perhaps this will.

This is a joke!! - *the mid forties wife decides that her body shape needs some effort and signs on at the local gym. She returns from her first visit, pulls herself up to her full height and narrowest perspectives as she mirror gazes her reflection.*

In walks the husband who says "How was the gym dear"; The wife replies 'very, very good. My new instructor said I have the bust of a twenty eight year old. The husband grunts and says "what about your forty five year old arse? With a shrug of the head the wife says, "Oh -we didn't talk about you at all".

When the storyline moves to the unexpected we laugh at ourselves first and the story- teller second. Here-in lies the power of humour. What did the joke teller get out of the exchange? People who heard the story laughed, they thought well of the story-teller. Good even smutty fun, perhaps at somebody's expense. In mixed company of forty five year olds the girls would relate to the joke element – the J factor, whilst overweight lads in the same company would register the niggle – N factor in the story. Making people laugh is a self-esteem builder for the story-teller and for as long as the **n J n J** majors on the non-threatening part of the joke, all is well. Humour and funny people help make the world a better place and long may it continue.

However there is a dark side to NjNj, niggle joke. Game playing jokers who need the personal attention and the associated power will say anything for a laugh. We were working with an operating crew at a workshop. One of the delegates arrived each morning to great laughter and several wise cracks about his lowly powered motorcycle and oversized crash helmet. When one joker started another joined in, this poor guy was the source of much laughter over a number of days. On the last morning of the programme the weather was awful, wind, horizontal rain and there was a quip-laden expectation of our bike rider arriving.

However the course organizer had received a message that John our bike rider would not be attending the programme. My colleague solemnly announced to the "Good morning delegates group" that John was hospitalised and would not attend. "John had parted company with his motorbike in the stormy weather". With lightning speed one joker said *"He was O.K. when he arrived at the hospital, but they had to break his fingers to detach his hands from the motor cycle"* Roaring laughter filled the room, but what expense the joke if the accident was serious?

Is this really funny?

Jokes are a way of centering attention on the speaker. Air-time occupied in the telling is rarely challenged. The speaker seems to cast a spell of silence over the listeners and if the joke hits the mark the purpose and intent is complete. Jokes dispensed at other people's expense have a subscript that is easily described. **I tell a story about you, everyone laughs with me and at you**. You feel awful, I feel good. When niggle joke becomes Nj, more niggle and wind-up than funny, the real undercover script of Nj is revealed. My real purpose is to wind you up, to make you feel bad, often with the same story. If the victim of a niggle joke reacts they deliver the pay-off to the game player. Game-on and standby for a subsequent re-run of exactly the same script. You can use your Thinkbox technique to counter the game. When Uh-Oh!! hits, don't react. Ask the game player, "Well, how was that for you dear?" then "Did that make you feel good? Oh I am pleased for you." Time and time again the game is played expecting to get the same pay off - a put you down – with laugh centered self esteem for the game player. Don't give the pay-off and the game will stop.

The game

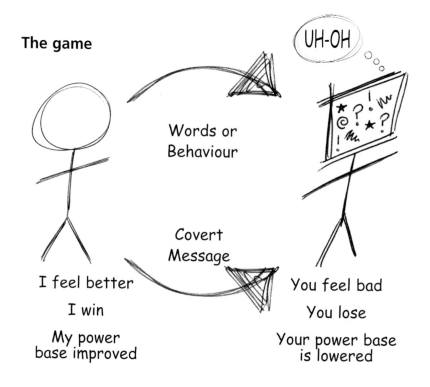

Words or
Behaviour

UH-OH

Covert
Message

I feel better

I win

My power
base improved

You feel bad

You lose

Your power base
is lowered

For most niggle – joke game players the **pay off** is that they feel good.
This leads us nicely on to the next game.

■ I improve my self-esteem when you do something wrong!!

"Look how good I am" – **LHGIAM**, is the payoff and the impact on the victim is "Look what you have done wrong". To explore **LHGIAM** lets consider the following example, the set for this drama is the works tour with old style boss. Two to three managers parade in front of the workforce and behind the big man who dully nitpicks his way around. Look at this, look at that, where is the last maintenance schedule for this machine. What was your efficiency on the back shift – questions asked to catch out the un-prepared and unwitting or as background data for the tongue lashing that comes next in the post tour performance review meeting.

Good Me   Poor you

With the big man operating in Isn't It Awful. **IIAWFUL** the managers sometimes move into **WCWBFThis**, 'Who can we blame for this' The Plant is operating below budget, why is output down"? "Well Boss it's really a mix factor, we keep selling low added value products at give away prices, here is the data to prove it". The sales manager says- If the quality on our high earners was better I could sell more". " Why is the quality poor" says the big man. "Because purchasing bought low grade components" says the next manager looking to pass the blame to someone else. A frustrated exchange of "Who can we blame for this" **WCWBFThis** then swallows up the next hour of expensive executive time.

"Who can we blame for this" – can debilitate a whole organisation. Here the last act may be redundancies, when years of possible progress have been lost by workers blaming managers, managers blaming unions, employees blaming unions and the idiot fringe blaming everyone, all with associated stories that are exchanged mostly within the separate tribes. **WCWBFThis** takes over and good people lose out.

■ Why do people play games?

People play games to maintain or develop **personal power** by fulfilling what they believe is their part in the **control and influence** drama. For example people who know there is personal power mileage in the message - **'you can't trust management'** - propagate the story with associated myths and war stories that support the script. Networks of No-trusters develop into real local power-bases. However, these soothsayers are really selling their view of the world with a script that meets their personal agenda. There can be a similar mechanism at work at Management board level where senior players blame the workforce as their alibi for poor performance and to survive this round of poor results. *WCWBFThis*, well if it wasn't for the workforce.

When Uh! Oh! hits an organisation the real character of people and teams comes through. If the corporate Uh! Oh! factor is perceived as a threat to the status of the power players then every power player who is operating beyond his level of competence behaves abnormally.

The Games people play are ready scripted in the Thinkbox, these are long held beliefs with supportive examples. By listening to the stories that people tell, you start to understand these scripts and hear the organisation's voice. This voice communicates what is important to the people in the organisation - understanding these messages can become the lift off point for change.

However, through its structure the Game is an undercover message and only when you understand the sub text will you surface the real intent of the communication. Communication moves out of Game mode when you have an Open discussion on the real issues that are driving the behaviour.

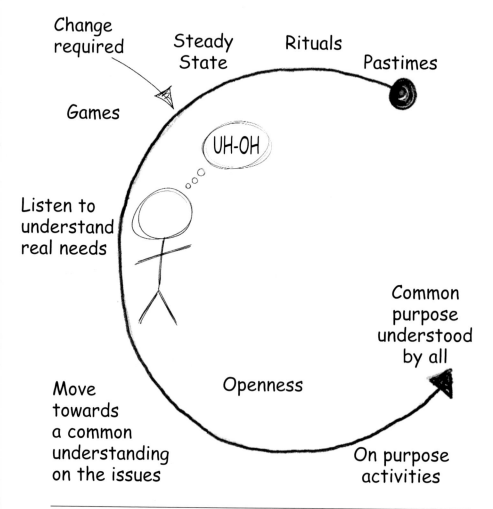

- When the tribal chief's sense danger they hand out the war paint - Zulu Zulu Zulu.

- Managers move into defensive positions.

- Employee tribes advance with loud noises.

- Power brokers distance to the hill tops leaving employees in the valley below.

- It can take years before they all meet in one place, and fact find through the smoke.

- When the risks escalate the lions wont be led by donkeys for too long.

- Move your organisation out of game mode and into Purposeful dialogue.

■ Playing games with Customer service

If we don't improve performance we may lose the contract. One of our Customers has suggested that you might be able to help. What do you suggest? A series of workshops followed where we engaged with the employees and listened to what they had to say. In summary this was the organisation's Game.

The combined logic of the employees on this issue can be summarized in one think bubble - Employee thinks - *Our managers screw us around, we can work a twelve hour shift and if we don't Meet the Plan then at 11.55 they tell us that we need to work on until sometimes 03.00 in the morning.*

The management logic bubble reads 'they haven't met the Plan, so we will make them work over!! Game on NIGYYSOB - **Now I have got you - you son of a bitch** - Pay back time.

Employee behaviours based on, we *know that if we don't deliver the Plan then our Customer, Big T, applies cost penalties to our company. They screw us around and so we screw them around.*

As facilitators of a change process we know we need to understand the organisation's inner voice. Very often fear and tribal history drive the real messages under-ground. Leaders then struggle with surface level difficulties because they don't understand the real messages and Employee needs.

When the Leaders understood the underlying reason for Employee behaviour the long-term performance problem on Customer Service was resolved within a week!!

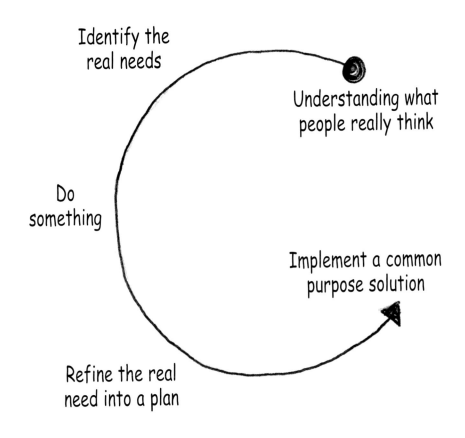

Identify the
real needs

Understanding what
people really think

Do
something

Implement a common
purpose solution

Refine the real
need into a plan

■ Organisational Uh! Oh!

Organisations have a collective memory bank, programmed through many heads and experienced history. If the organisation's existing life pattern - the corporate comfort zone - is disturbed by a market place change, a competitor, ownership or even a new boss or budget, the people in the organisation automatically react to the change and the whole organisation can move into Uh-Oh!! mode.

The methodology for measuring the degree of "out-of-control" in individuals can be used to evaluate organisations. Look around the boardroom and people-watch for changes in behaviour. When the steady state and predictable heart-beat of an established business is rumbled by an external influence the power players exhibit common behaviours.

Imagine the effect on the long-term manager with a hidden secret. Lets use Excel-dyslexia as an example, or a spelling default or a software phobia that has remained hidden from the eyes of the previous, long stay CEO. At the time when the new CEO is announced and even before she arrives our manager hits Uh-Oh!! How will this change affect me? I know that I am not as good as the others at learning or manipulating data. In the very next office sits the Technical Director who was fired in her last company by a new MD who understood that she wasn't very Techy. Her real forte was metallurgy and this was a plastics business. She hits Uh-Oh!! as well.

At the long Friday afternoon review meeting [or perhaps the must be in before everyone else start] that had its origins in the 1970's logic of the board work the longest hours – top team set an example, Uh! Oh! pervades the air. Most people have a number of managerial demerits and there is nothing like the new boss effect to start the worry beads rattling. If you now connect these, Uh! Oh! brain waves from everyone's forehead into a main-board-mini-circuit then the team who are charged with running the ship can be debilitated. Listen to the stories that people tell each other, pension calculations, severance models or the headhunter called last week, all reflecting the degree of Uh-Oh!!

Lets pause for a rational thought; the new boss hasn't arrived yet. We have already taken out the - **what will she expect check list** - and identified glaring blanks in mental tick boxes. These fears are then amplified by the late CEO's leaving do and the new CEO's early days in post. The Uh-Oh!! factor grows with each day.

Whilst the power players introvert into their shells, they perhaps fail to register that if the business requires anything more complicated that a mechanistic change then the new CEO will probably not know which end of the stick to pick up. She will go through the new boss routines and send subtle, irrelevant signals and territorial messages. A procession of power brokers file through her door and in the ensuing ninety minutes, amplify their strengths, do a bit-of-bonding and explain the shortcomings of the last three CEO's and the rest of the board. Most of these messages are of course sub textualised under "You will probably find this out for yourself". Brains become

Where did I
leave those
buns?

numbed by this process and the early board meetings are edgy. Sharp professional exchanges dominate as people redesign their work mask to match what they believe is the new leaders behaviour set and agenda.

If you introduce a new business dynamic to this equation like a new budget or reporting regime - standby for the bang!! Highly paid long stay Managers and Directors can quickly convert Thinkbox Uh-Oh!! into irrational behaviour. Having fed the hidden secret mind monster large buns- with sleep deprivation and the rattle of worry beads, just a little more negative energy can tip the balance. When the Thinkbox is on the edge even the static from a minor event can overload the system. In Uh-Oh!! mode the pressure that we inflict on ourselves through uncontrolled imagination is mind-boggling.

Our analysis of our short-comings may be accurate, but if the hidden secret is converted into an improvement agenda and action then the new boss Uh-Oh!! effect translates into a growth and development opportunity. Whenever a new boss arrives or even a new powerful board member, just remember one powerful key message.

There is nothing like a little pressure to expose real character.

When the risks are low and the people in the business are not under threat many management meetings resemble tea parties. Routine data is explored, excuses accepted for non-performance and what goes around comes around again if the agenda ever reaches it.

If you are charged with helping change an existing power base or established work order, make sure that you are earthed. As your ideas stand tall, the lightning tension will strike you first. Latent energy stored in old and outdated ways of working always strikes back when disturbed.

Under the table issues

Cost down plans v Board room bonus payments

Self important leaders who add no real value

Overtime and redundancy rackets

LIFO - Status quo - Safety manipulators using Safety as a political tool

We know where your car is

■ How do you cope with power base changes?

Your organisation will be subject to ongoing change and as a moving part in that organisation, so will you. Business and life pressures will always impact on your immediate work environment, but the real challenge is when a powerful force starts to move in your life and work orbit. Let's define what this powerful force can be, with a message that is both simple and complex.

Simply stated; *anything that You perceive to be a challenge or threat to your Personal Power and Influence is a power base change*, how you deal with either real or imagined impacts dictates the forces that come into play.

In each of us there is a natural Uh-Oh!! threshold that determines how we react to the unexpected. The more exposure that we have to change the more accustomed our Thinkbox becomes to managing it. Even the change hardy veteran needs to recognize that there are limits to what we can accommodate.

Now is this how the equation adds up? With a Change Gene-bank, hand me down, ancestral or message from Grandma factor [G] *plus* What ever has happened to you in your life, the changes that you have coped with and survived, [H] *plus* the higher the change order that you have experienced [N]. Then to become an ACE changemaster we will need to combine and develop the factors in the following equation.

$$G + H + N = ACE$$

| Gene Factor | What's Happened to you | High Order Problems Resolved | Emotional Wave Surfer |

There is an argument that if you want to be able to cope with change at an intuitive level your life experience requires you to move through significant turbulent change, and at the end of this process look back on the Uh-Oh!! period with a considered smile and a satisfying and refreshing intake of air. With an increasing change management capability you will be ready to cope with higher order change or simply whatever Uh-Oh's!! life throws at you.

Moving to a new performance level in coping with change requires a similar break through for the experienced as for the naïve. We all go through the Uh-Oh!! barrier on the low order issues of change, wobble a little - then self correct and stay upright. Using the new Thinkbox processes we control and with ongoing practice absorb external Change energy. Then using new change-managing-mechanisms will help us cope and move forward.

Change leaders thrive here

Make sure that you understand who the enemy is before going to war

Our experience with many organisations is that rock logic, captured in old work practices and agreements becomes a game scenario for the power brokers. With every old agreement comes the associated war stories that justify in someone's head why they should apply this old logic to today's agenda. The older the organisation the thicker the tome of understandings. I was once faced with a Leading hand who produced a yellow and brown edged sheet of A4 dated 1939 as proof that he was right. Fifty years before this exchange he probably was, when the context and purpose of the agreement made sense, he was not for persuading that time had moved on. Rock logic, tablets of stone that can develop a following if it suits the purpose of the person peddling the messages.

Similarly Management and leadership teams can rely on what worked in the past in a similar way to the Union power brokers. Both can be summarised as - the gospel according to me - with ninety percent plus of the resistance to change at the top of the organisations power groups. Manager, Union, Employee teams all respond to changes in a similar way with the established power players resisting change the most.

In many organisations both Management and Unions draw battle lines over holy cows like, our right to manage, last in first out, status quo, with fifty two versions of what the words on the page meant or mean. Years of activity and negative energy devoted to issues that don't really affect the average employee. The games become deep and the consequences chilling. Good people lose their jobs as the inevitable outcome of a Game ridden environment. Anything goes, overtime cuts result in Safety restrictions, overtime conjuring through manning and training rackets. Agreements that mean the company have to waste money on uneccessary manning levels. Redundancy rackets, "close the place see if I care, give me the payoff" messages echo across mess rooms and canteens. Hello is any one looking after my long term future here - hell no, we are at war over double time for the 27th December that we now decide is Christmas day - true story.

Management teams feed the Bear who in turn writes their bonus cheques. Quote- 'If they want me to stand on one leg and salute the American flag I will do it' - no hopers queue up like nodding dogs and become clones of the new boss's recipe for personal gain. Employees become really confused when the top dog does new tricks that they don't understand and are probably the exact opposite of last years route to survival.

Stop the games we want to stay on, probably reflects the average Employee's thinking. But unless the voice of the majority is mobilised the power brokers keep doing the same old things. Management, Union and Employee dinosaurs who make Barney Rubble seem like an innovator.

In this type of business the in-fighting can become so intense and pre-occupying that the competitive world quickly outpaces the dinosaurs within. Whilst the power brokers tramp through the same old arguments and tribal wars their competitors are both eating their lunch and dining out with their Customers. The rock logic squad become uncompetitive and this country is littered with closed companies that failed to address the issue of change early enough. Organisations laden with really busy people hypnotised by internal conflicts and much too preoccupied to notice what was going on in the big world market place outside.

Name the games, decide what your Employee Purpose really is, have all work teams describe the path to a more secure future, then move towards it together, as one work community, with simple logic loops owned by all.

A war vintage Eastern German rolling mill, re-energised through the following Purpose Statement- **We will retain the maximum number of competitive jobs, through Customer service, from a plant that we can be proud of** . Simple messages that all employees articulate, usually work best.

This is not a soft and fluffy process. When an organisation describes its people Purpose and culture as world class, everyone needs to change and upgrade their personal performance. Can any organisation survive in the long term without the attitude shift that aligns employees with the best in their industry or market sector? Whilst the facilties may not be world class can we settle for anything less than a world class attitude and best of my ability from our people?

We need to change now if our country is not to become a series of golf courses where our young people caddy and green keep because they can't afford to play and our forty five year olds watch television for the whole of the waking week. Addressing the competitive issues of three years from now should become an organisation's Purpose and thinking theme with the full cooperation of all employees.

Openess-honesty-loyalty-trust and other working together words that describe how we behave now as opposed to the game ridden world of yesterday. These relationships will characterize the successful organisations of the future.

- We are only capable of working towards a future that we can describe.

- Board rooms, branch meetings, management and union power brokers, often describe life on different planets.

- Really listening to each other is rare but has to be the start of crafting a common purpose.

- The leaders role is to create a framework for a **common Employee purpose.**

- Identify the real needs.

- Let the front line teams describe how we can.

◼ Most external forces don't really impact or influence what is really important to us

Every time we manage Uh-Oh!! we learn a little but stay in control. Positive energy released to balance negative external force is calibrated by us. When change hardened and active we will expend little proactive energy unless the external force impacts on something that is really important to us. To achieve the best energy usage we need to identify the limits that are we prepared to go to, to defend what in my experience are the base line issues like fairness and integrity and playing within the rules. These 'Importants' generate an enormous level of individual and organisational energy, but the identification of *'what is important to you is the key'*. Give your 'importants' a 1,2,3,4,5 listing, having focussed on them you will then automatically align your energy drive and effort towards them.

Most of the over promoted in your organisation know in their heart and head that they cannot cope with business challenge or change. In a Thinkbox context they have been working on the edge for some time. As they move through working life and skirt the edge of change their internal Uh-Oh!! factor increases. Imagine a Thinkbox wobble factor that they only just manage to work within and remain upright.

Working in this way produces stress and strain and requires energy to maintain a secretive work mask or curtain that only the Thinkbox owner can see behind. But real bangs occur when the person behind the mask feels that they are about to be exposed, or outed as someone that they are pretending not to be. When this occurs the defensive energy can be both hostile and aggressive, major mood swings with the odd tantrum thrown in. Internal fear energy combines with an external change challenge with a resultant-Thinkbox bang!! Analysing -*"Why do I feel this way"*- will usually circle around one issue – **Fear of!!** By balancing the natural primal energy in this equation-from being afraid of losing something on the one side with the thinking response of, so what if I do? The equation becomes simpler. Pre-programme your Thinkbox, identify before hand what is important to you. What do you really value, **when it comes down to the last three to five choices of what you really, really want**-what will they be? By identifying and centering your life around this Real Purpose you build a powerful defence field within which you can manage the forces of change. Against the really important factors in your life, most of the people, team and organisational power plays become low order impacts from which you learn, grow and increase your change management capability **Uh-Oh!! then equals; from this I will learn.**

When Uh-Oh!! hits think it through, and filter your response by letting through information that is important to you.

For me it's family and friends and adding value through the people that I am privileged to work with. Asking 'What is important to me?" triggers a hard wired Thinkbox response with a powerful, emotional connect with people who are here and a few who are no longer with us. If when you ask the question- **What is important to Me?** you connect with similar ideas then you are right in the middle of Uh-Oh!! right now, you may be on the edge of your emotional wave and you can learn to enjoy it.

Move, breathe, look up, then choose a happy memory to re-connect with, whenever your Thinkbox takes you that way. Your mind can whiz through generations and with each mini connection reinforce the network and help you understand what is important to you.

Through an understanding of the Uh-Oh!! effect you can begin to manage the change process for your-self, then with opportunity, experience and practice you will move to a higher Thinkbox order. This can help you make this life a better place for you and those who share it with you. Will we also contribute to a higher thinking order for those who follow? Just calibrate the Thinkbox-change coming-advanced warning mechanism - Uh-Oh!! then engage your real time brain to manage the old networks. When the Uh-Oh!! effect becomes a signal for the new, you learn that without it you can only stay the same.

Now this is Personal-when Uh-Oh!! hits-within milliseconds, you have options. We hope that the thoughts on these pages connect for you and help you make a better choice.

- Enjoy today, the weeks, the year, this life.

- Create order in your Thinkbox through practice ahead of the time.

- Center the order on what's important to you.

- Describe your happy bunny sense in words, sights, sounds and feelings.

- As you reinforce this Thinkbox data today you dilute old, rock logic data.

- Know your body trigger.

- Sense changes by the way you feel.

- Know that when you manage Uh-Oh moments you learn.

- Choose to sense your happy bunny mode right now.

- Make this a better place for you and for me.

The credits are all yours

To those who have walked the earth before us, and to

Rachel and Anthony for turning the water into wine

Lynch and Kordis who wrote Strategy of the Dolphin

Spencer Johnson for Who moved my cheese-Yes or No and Present

Granville for eating the cheese

Hughie for breaking down on Ballachulish Bridge to watch the Ark Royal

David Bohn for writing Thought as a system

Smith San, Burnand San and Thorby San for mega change the movie

Jim Mowatt for lessons on lightning conducting and tight rope walking

Ian Dhu, John Meffen, Hugh Cark, George Haggart, Alan McLean for lessons in the ancient Highland art of treacle walking

Laurence Faircloth for seeing the light, Mel, Eddie and Jeff for putting the fires out

Chris for hypnotherapy, Pauline for practising it and Moira for being fine

The Larkins for writing Communicating change

Phil, Nigel, Pat, Gwyn and the Bosch squad

Mr Edwards for sponsoring the middle muddle insights

Mike Harris for Logan and teaching buffaloes to fly in downtown Kentucky

Simon Harris, David Underwood, the 'A' team, Deborah, Ruth, Lyndon

Stuart Hyde for seeing London from Ilkley Moor

To the Hettstedt squad for greeting an islander

John Brown for describing something different at Weston

Adrian Burleton for flying high on dialogue and Patchway

Norman for being a peacock in the land of the penguins

Rick Maurer for writing Beyond the Wall of Resistance

To John Carter and the West Yorkshire team for bringing it to life

Dorothy Jongeward for writing Born to Win

To West Yorks Admin team for the message 'only losers play games'

To Jen the Cartref maker extraordinaire in Neath, Alness, Fort William and Newport

To our No1, No2, No3 and to our girls and boys and to those who will follow them

To those who will walk this earth after us

■ Moving to a higher order

On October 3rd 2005 we attended the funeral of Martin Claase a young family friend who had grown up with our children in Scotland. Martin had died as a result of a reaction to a known allergy as he returned from holiday for his final term at University.

In thought bubbles and Thinkboxing we have used the wave model in a number of ways and Martin created our emotional tsunami. The church was charged with emotion as we thought through our loss and recalled good times with Martin .

Martin's family had decided that the day would be a celebration of his life and that we should reflect the fact that Martin made us smile in the service. Through the eulogy and messages from the Priest I think we did our best to fulfil our ideas that we should smile and remember and to a degree this worked.

The church service was followed by a short but complicated journey to Logie Churchyard which sits in the shadow of the Wallace monument in Bridge of Allan. A really beautiful final resting place that snuggles into the hills . Five hundred people shared a mild autumn day as the sun shone but the mood of the gathering was predictably sombre as we all made our way to the graveside.

The Priest was ready to say the last prayers for Martin and as the bearers were called, Gareth, Martin's elder brother, spoke quietly to the Priest to advise that the car carrying Martin's school friends had detoured to somewhere and that we might need to wait for them to arrive.

Now the Priest had met Uh-Oh a few times during that morning and he was just about to meet it again as the delay grew into many minutes. Gareth remained strong through the wait with the message that Martin's friends would never forgive themselves if they did not help Martin to his resting place. But the tension grew as the minutes elapsed. Then suddenly, a few hundred meters away the churchyard gates opened and through the gate came a car load of Martin's friends.

They ran towards the assembled hundreds with a style that came straight out of a film set, it could have been Duncan from Monarch of the Glen, or Forest Gump, or perhaps even the ambling charge of the Scots in Braveheart. Arms flailing with oversteer on the corners as they sprinted towards us. They almost screeched to a breathless halt as the Priest's right hand man called their names and we all said goodbye to Martin's body but in a way we had just reconnected with his spirit.

Gareths eulogy had recalled that Martin had attended his final day at school in a Gorilla costume - everyone laughed. If he had scripted his funeral he would have planned it this way. As his school mates charged frantically through the cemetry gates the assembled hundreds were only a sobering step away from giving a round of applause.

None of us will ever forget Martin and Martin's funeral will become part of our history, it will be a story that we will retell and retell. Perhaps these memories will never die as we tell our young one's the story and the messages from Martin's life. If you drive through Stirling and look towards the Wallace monument then a few hundred meters to the south lies Logie Church yard. As you navigate your mind in that general direction, think of Martin and smile.

Our ideas pop quickly, spontaneously, but you almost need to be prepared in the right way before they can have the impact that you were hoping for. We had all been describing to ourselves a celebration of Martin's life and his humour and his smile and we still miss all of these. Yet the Churchyard event pulled this all together for us. We really did smile with a today event moving us to a higher order.

Think of Martin, say thank you for the memory, move, breathe and look up and then smile.

Notes

Notes

Published by New Era
Thinkboxing@2020change.co.uk